# Churches and Chapels of Kirklees

"We shape our buildings,
then our buildings shape us"

Churchill

# Churches and Chapels of Kirklees

With Photographs by the Author

A Ronald Bielby

Directorate of Educational Services
Kirklees Metropolitan Council
Headquarters
Princess Alexandra Walk
Huddersfield HD1 2SU
1978
ISBN 0 9502568 5 4

Printed by
H Charlesworth & Co Ltd
England

## CONTENTS

The roundel of the cover is part of a brass plaque in the entrance hall of Huddersfield Library, which reads: "On this site formerly stood the Ramsden Street Independent Chapel. Opened December 28 1825. Closed December 17 1933" (see page 80)

*Illustration 1 (Frontispiece) Dewsbury* All Saints, *the Mother of us all, the oldest church in Kirklees, believed to have been founded in A.D. 627 by Paulinus, the first Archbishop of York.*

# INTRODUCTORY

## 1. THE SCOPE OF THIS SURVEY

The churches and chapels of Kirklees are homes of congregations; they have been and are places for worship, and not centres of pilgrimage or monuments of ecclesiastical architecture. There is no cathedral among them, though there are delightful buildings which are important and typical of their sort. Belonging to many centuries, they exemplify a development which extends over the whole country, particular buildings affording excellent illustrations of the various stages in the history of religious architecture as it has served the day-to-day needs of ordinary folk.

It is important to include in the story Free Church and Roman Catholic buildings; the former because in our industrial valleys chapels, more often than not, came before the present local churches and are more characteristic of the landscape, the latter because in them is expressed more clearly the current direction of church design in response to newer liturgical thinking.

Broadly speaking, Anglican churches can be grouped into four main categories, all found in Kirklees; there are four categories, too, in Free Church buildings. By looking at particular buildings as belonging to one or other of these categories we are able better to appreciate their places in the historical development of our area, and recognise, too, their strengths and weaknesses in the face of the social conditions of our own day.

The following brief statement of these categories is filled out in later chapters where examples are described. It will, of course, be recognised that churches, like houses, undergo modifications and expansions as needs arise or fashion dictates, so that buildings as they are now may differ considerably, especially in their internal arrangements, from the intentions of those who first erected them.

### The Established Church

(i) *The pre-Reformation two-room type*

There are nine such churches in Kirklees, all retaining a clear chancel/nave division (the two "rooms"), in every case marked by a change in roof heights. The nave was the people's part of the church and served all the purposes of the village hall of today; the chancel was the priest's part, separated by the screen. The individual's worship was largely a private activity within the public setting of the mass.

(ii) *The post-Reformation one-room type*

With the Reformation came a stress on preaching; the pulpit, not the altar, became the focus of worship. People were to hear and participate, for the service was in English, not Latin; the *one* room was for both minister and people, the old hierarchy disappearing. Existing churches were modified (with much wanton destruction) in internal arrangements. When new buildings were needed the classical style provided a suitable medium to express the new thinking. There are several classical churches of this period in Kirklees. Here, too, should be placed the several "Waterloo" churches.

2 *Emley* St Michael, *a landmark much as it is now for over 500 years. The two "rooms" – the chancel with the priest's door and the nave with the people's door – are marked by the change in roof levels.*

(iii) *The Gothic Revival: the two-room type restored*

In the 1830s the Oxford Movement gave fresh prominence to the eucharist, and, in seeking to revive old ritual, revived also the Gothic style, "the only true Christian architecture". Most of the Anglican churches in Kirklees are nineteenth century Gothic, differing internally from the Gothic of the Middle Ages by the visual stress on the altar (the vista), by the use of steps instead of a screen to separate the chancel from the nave, and by the introduction of stalls for a surpliced choir in the chancel.

(iv) *The modern one-room type*

Most recent church building is contemporary in architectural style, avoiding the backward-looking associations of Gothic. The increasing democratisation of all aspects of life has given added strength to the new Liturgical Movement which spread from Continental Catholicism, and this has affected both Anglican and Free Church building in Kirklees – as at the Church of Christ the King, Battyeford.

**The Free Churches**

(i) *Meeting-houses and Preaching-houses*

It was not till the Toleration Act of 1689 that Dissenters' places of worship were granted legal recognition. Till then, with the exception of a few years during the Commonwealth, the official view was that a country could have, indeed must have, one common form of religion and that every citizen owed allegiance to the national church. Early meeting-houses (and, with the Methodists, preaching-houses) were domestic and vernacular in character, humble rather than ugly. Some fine examples still exist in Kirklees, though older buildings are fast disappearing.

(ii) *The "Messiah" Chapels*

Once the organ was approved it was given pride of place in many chapels, towering, with the choir, above the centrally placed pulpit. Anglican choirs were divided to ensure a vista of the altar; no such requirement affected nineteenth century chapels which grew in size, matching in style the organ-laden town halls. Performances of Handel's *Messiah* and anniversary services with their singing dominated the design of buildings. Kirklees still has chapels which tell this story. In later classical-style buildings denominations vied with each other in architectural extravagance.

(iii) *The Gothic Revival type*

Classical styles were long retained in Nonconformity, a sign of difference from the Established Church, but towards the end of the nineteenth century Gothic styles, now freed from links with the Oxford Movement, became acceptable. In many cases the Messiah-chapel type of interior was installed in

3 *The vernacular: Wooldale* Meeting House of the Society of Friends (Quakers), *erected in the lifetime of their founder George Fox (1624-91) and said to have been visited by him.*

a Gothic shell, choir stalls and organ filling the chancel area. In some Methodist chapels the two-room Anglican layout was adopted and still remains.

(iv) *The modern ecumenical style*

The Liturgical Movement which affected Anglican building, in turn spread to the Free Churches. The new stress on the one-ness of all the people of God found architectural expression whether because of fashion or out of conviction as a positive choice. The New North Road Baptist Church in Huddersfield adds to the new style its own special emphasis on the Ministry of the Word and on believers' baptism.

This survey of churches and chapels in Kirklees does not seek to replace the pamphlets and brochures which individual churches produce about their own story (and there are some excellent ones); the intention is to enable each to be set in the one story of a development which is common to the whole country and exemplified in Kirklees. To illustrate this development selection has been necessary, especially from the many nineteenth century buildings, and an arbitrary element inevitably enters, for many not mentioned could equally well have served our purpose. Nevertheless, the hope is that readers of this study may be able, from it, to understand better how any particular church in which they are interested came to be planned as it is, and how it fits into the whole story of buildings for the worship of God.

# THE ESTABLISHED CHURCH

## 2. PRE-REFORMATION CHURCHES

### How old is a church?

It depends on what you mean by "church". In this survey a building is meant: you *go* to church. But in *New Testament* usage a church is a group of Christians who worship together, a congregation, and this prior meaning still remains. A church building may be demolished and a new one erected, but in a real sense the "church" continues, for continuity does not necessarily reside in buildings. In Huddersfield, for instance, the present parish church dates from 1836; it is not ancient, there were two earlier buildings. But the "church" dates from about 1100 A.D. It is the *parish*, not the building, which is ancient.

The Yorkshire Archaeological Society has published a *Map of Ancient Parishes and Chapelries* based, for our area, on Henry Teesdale's map of Yorkshire of 1828. Eleven parishes with as many chapelries cover Kirklees. There were therefore eleven churches and, of these, sufficient of nine remain as part of present buildings to justify their claim to be ancient. Obviously

4 *Batley* All Saints *is one of the least changed of our ancient churches. The Perpendicular tower is unique in Kirklees. Inside there are parclose screens, effigies, old glass and a rood staircase.*

5 *Batley* All Saints. *The tower was designed for refuge and defence. The parapet was corbelled out so that raiders could be attacked by bow fire or stones through the gaps — a thirteenth century* machicolated *parapet.*

there is an arbitrary element here. Mirfield *St Mary* is excluded because the surviving tower of the medieval church is not incorporated in Sir George Gilbert Scott's building of 1871, but Kirkheaton *St John* is included because the Beaumont Chapel (at the east end of the north aisle) and the tower were saved from the great fire of 1886 to be incorporated in the new building of 1887-8. The least changed of our ancient churches are Batley *All Saints* and Emley *St Michael*, but even where there are considerable nineteenth century restorations there is usually a place for old relics, as in the "museum corner" at Birstall *St Peter* which, except for the tower, was rebuilt 1863-70.

The nine "ancient" churches are Almondbury, Batley, Birstall, Dewsbury, Emley, Hartshead, Kirkburton, Kirkheaton and Thornhill, the church at Dewsbury (*All Saints*) being the Mother church. The tradition is that Paulinus, the first Archbishop of York, was its founder in 627 A.D. The Saxon parish of Dewsbury covered 400 square miles and extended beyond the boundaries of Kirklees and Calderdale to meet the parish of Whalley.

Of the eleven ancient chapelries within the Kirklees area there is no surviving building though the old term "chapel" for a place of worship subordinate to the parish church, or in some way private, remains at Cleckheaton *Whitechapel*, where the chapel of c.1130 was rebuilt in 1706 and again in 1821, and is now a parish church. Three of the eleven chapelries were in the parish of Huddersfield: Longwood, Scammonden, Slaithwaite; one in Almondbury: Meltham; one shared by Huddersfield and Almondbury: Marsden; two in Birstall: Cleckheaton, Liversedge; one in Kirkburton: Holmfirth; one in Thornhill: Flockton; and two in High Hoyland (itself not in Kirklees): Cumberworth and West Clayton.

**A Victorian restoration**

Ancient churches have seen two major changes in the requirements of worship, one during the turbulent period of the Reformation ending in the slow working out of the implications of the Elizabethan Settlement, the other following the Oxford Movement of the 1830s with its new stress on ritual; both involved considerable internal re-arrangements. But what of the actual buildings themselves? The gradual extensions and enrichments of the Middle Ages were halted at the Reformation though, inevitably, from time to time individual buildings needed repair. Dewsbury *All Saints*, for instance, being

6 *Hartshead* St Peter*: a copy of an old photograph taken from* Brighouse: its Scenery and Antiquities *by G. Hepworth (1885) showing the church before the restoration of 1881. Compare porch, windows and roof with the next Illustration.*

7 *Hartshead* St Peter. *"Mostly neo-Norman of 1881", says Pevsner. However, the tower is Norman, and the inner doorway and chancel arch. The yew of Illustration 6, further abbreviated, still stands, dead as it was then.*

unsafe, was partly rebuilt in 1767 and this accounts for the curious mixture of classical and Gothic elements in the tower.

But the nineteenth century was the greatest period of restoration, necessary renewal of fabric often being made an occasion to meet the requirements of the new ritual. Consequently much of what we see now in our "ancient" churches, both inside and out, is Victorian. We illustrate by a close look at Hartshead *St Peter*. The before-and-after photographs show external changes. It is hard to imagine the earlier interior of box pews and wooden pillars, with a west gallery for musicians and singers, and later on an organ; harder still to imagine its medieval days.

**Reminders of ancient practice**

Before there were any churches in Kirklees there was Christian teaching. Itinerant monks preached and baptised, sometimes in the open air, sometimes under the shelter of simple wood and thatch structures. Are there links between these early days and buildings now standing? There is a good deal of conjecture about the beginnings of individual churches, and a strong desire to establish antiquity. Can it really be that Dewsbury owes its name to Paulinus

8 *Hartshead* St Peter. *The restoration has been sympathetically carried out; only the chancel arch in the photograph is genuine Norman. The earlier flat ceiling, sash windows, two-decker pulpit, high pews and galleries, and, most important, the wooden pillars have all gone. We use the word "restoration", but no medieval church would ever have looked like this.*

who established "God's Fort" there? The Domesday Book refers to *Deusberia*, and *Deus* is Latin for "God", but the linguistic point is a highly doubtful one. There is more concrete evidence in the discovery of preaching crosses (to be distinguished from later memorial crosses). These exist, or something like them, at Birstall, Dewsbury, Kirkburton, Kirkheaton and Thornhill, though mostly as fragments.

Crosses were erected to mark the places where preaching and the celebration of the mass took place. At Kirkburton, what is believed to be a preaching cross – in fact, a crucifix – has been re-assembled and stands now in the church. The pieces were found when the chancel walls were being repaired, one piece in rubble in 1850, others twenty years later, as though they had been incorporated when a permanent place of worship was erected, but exact dating is difficult. The ninth century is claimed, even several centuries earlier. Factors which are relevant, we are told, are the long garment (not just a loin cloth), the length of the hair, the erect posture – Christ "reigning from the tree" rather than suffering, and the spread feet (four nails, not three). The figure of Christ stands with arms outspread, as if to embrace all mankind.

When a shelter was first put over the portable altar set up at the foot of the preaching cross it was for the priest's benefit; later the people built their own protection from northern weather. From this, it has been suggested sprang the medieval custom of divided responsibility for the structure of the church, the two rooms. The altar house, the chancel, was the priest's responsibility; the nave, the people's meeting place, was the parishioners' responsibility; chancel and nave were separate. In many instances the dividing wall, the chancel arch, proved to be one of the most permanent features of the whole building — as at Hartshead.

It requires an act of imagination to appreciate the colour and richness of the parish church as villagers must have seen it. Unless a castle or manor house was nearby it was probably the only stone building; village homes were of mud and wattle, or of timber and thatch. But the nave of the church, uncluttered with pews, was their own, spacious, dry and colourful.

Colourful, because every craft was brought to the service of the church: painting, glass work, wood and stone carving. Alas, we look in vain in Kirklees for wall paintings though traces were found during nineteenth century restorations. But most of our ancient churches contain some old glass, in spite of much damage in the sixteenth and seventeenth centuries. Some was retrieved and replaced as best could be: there is, for instance, a recognisable bit of a crucifixion scene at Batley *All Saints*. Several whole windows remain almost complete, though with lost colour, including the great Jesse window at Thornhill *St Michael*.

The Jesse window is of special interest because it reveals how the medieval mind interpreted a passage from *Isaiah* which for the early Church was a prophecy of Christ's incarnation:

> There shall come forth a rod out of the stem of Jesse, and a Branch shall grow out of his roots: And the spirit of the Lord shall rest upon him, . . . (*Isaiah* 11. 1-2.)

There was a simple literalism in the depiction of a vine rising from the sleeping Jesse, the father of David. Its branches support Jesse's descendants, a veritable family tree of Christ, and at its highest point, dominating the whole, are shown the Virgin Mary with the infant Jesus and Christ in glory. The photograph includes only four of the 24 lights of the window; the two lower lights depict Jesse and the tree issuing from him; the two upper lights, David playing his harp and Solomon with a model of his Temple. This window carries an inscription which confirms that the chancel (sanctuary plus choir) was the special concern of the clergy:

> Pray for ye gude pperity, mercy and grace of Robert ffrost ccellor to ye redoubted Prince Arthur, 1st sonne of King Henry VIj, who

***9 & 10*** *(opposite)*

*Kirkburton* All Hallows. *The reassembled cross, believed to be an Anglo-Saxon preaching cross, has interlaced decoration at its lower end (shown on a larger scale in Illustration 10). The cross now stands by the chancel arch on the south side of the nave.*

was late parson of this church who hathe made new est window, and also clerestoried and archede this choir; finished ye yeare of grace 1499.

Restoration work was done on this window from 1877 to 1879; during World War II its glass was taken out and stored in a local mine.

At a time when books were few and expensive, the ability to read rare, and when services were in Latin, the church taught very largely by festivals and by visual aids — the paintings on the walls, the windows, the church furnishings and the many religious symbols. In particular the placing of the font — near the people's door to indicate that by baptism you enter the Church — was itself religiously significant. You were reminded every time you passed it of the promises made for you. Fonts may themselves carry symbols of the faith; they are not infrequently retained from an earlier building and so are older than the church itself. The font at Cleckheaton *Whitechapel* is one such, Norman in a nineteenth century building.

But the chief reminder of ancient practice and attitudes is the unchanged groundplan of churches, the division into chancel and nave. The separating chancel arch was filled with a screen made usually of wood: it excluded the laity from the mysteries; they were to be onlookers, not participants. The Church consisted of clergy and laity. There were, of course, functional reasons for screens as there were later for high pews: for one thing they were draught-excluders in days before central heating. But more: clergy from monastic houses would use the chancels of their churches every day, several times a day. When, on Sundays, villagers attended, they were spectators of what more often went on without them. To be present was the important thing; their private prayers, their private devotion and aspiration, if not always articulate, was part of their life. And this established the pattern. If they made their communion at all, and this was rare, it was only "in one kind", the bread or wafer.

The two-room division of the church remained through all the architectural changes of the pre-Reformation period. But there was elaboration, and the division came to symbolise, too, the hierarchical pattern of feudal society as chantry chapels and family memorials multiplied and interiors became increasingly compartmentalised. The several chapels, each with its altar, were in their turn divided off by lesser screens (parclose screens), and in them chantry priests would "chant" masses for the repose of the souls of their benefactors and their families. The foundation of chantries was often linked with the creation of chantry schools, the priests teaching in their spare time. Not all chantry chapels were sited inside parish churches. In Almondbury, for instance, there were three in the church and one which occupied several successive sites in St Helen's Gate. To this latter King James's School looks

*11 (opposite)*

*Batley* All Saints. *The rescued medieval glass in the window is part of a crucifixion scene. The figure is probably the penitent thief.*

back for its real beginning though it had to be re-founded when chantries were suppressed.

In the fifteenth century rood lofts became common — galleries several feet wide above the chancel screen, sometimes called the rood-screen because a rood (a crucifix usually flanked by the figures of Mary the mother of Jesus, and John the Evangelist) surmounted it. The rood loft, approached by a stairway, was commonly used by church musicians. Above the screen, on the wall above the chancel arch, there would be a Doom picture, showing the joys of heaven and the agonies of hell. And all these things were opportunities for artistry and craftsmanship. The appeal was more to the eye than to the ear.

The Reformers destroyed roods and figures and cared little for screens. Some remote churches in the countryside escaped most of this destruction but Kirklees has no original chancel screen or rood though some parclose screens are retained — as at Batley. At Batley, too, there is a rood staircase at the south side in the thickness of the wall, discovered when the church was restored in 1873 and now leading nowhere.

Some of our more recent churches have roods mounted on rood beams though they are often without screens. In seeking to restore something of the mystery, numinous quality and devotion of ancient worship they remind us of what was the norm in church furnishing in pre-Reformation days. A different and interesting twentieth century development is that of multi-purpose halls, as though economic necessity were compelling a return, if only partially, to the unity of life of the Middle Ages when all aspects of communal life were centred in the parish church.

*12 (opposite)*

*Thornhill* St Michael. *Part of the great east window, a much restored tree of Jesse, a family tree of Christ. David Rex, with his harp, is upper left; Solomon, holding a model of his Temple, is upper right.*

*13 (page 22)*

*Emley* St Michael. *The "tulip" font, which stands at the back of the nave, dates from the end of the seventeenth century. It is not as old as the church; an earlier font has disappeared.*

*14 (page 23)*

*Almondbury* All Hallows. *The three-tiered font cover is Perpendicular in style as is the church itself. It was carefully restored in 1874.*

ET INCLINA COR

15 *Cleckheaton* Whitechapel. *The Norman font is more valued now than it has ever been. It was used as a pedestal for the font of the 1706 building, it has been buried, now it stands on a new pedestal, concrete evidence of the antiquity of the chapelry.*

16 *Batley* All Saints. *Iron mouldings to the same pattern have been used to replace damaged woodwork in the old parclose screen of the present Lady Chapel. There is the occasional mis-match.*

17 *Batley* All Saints. *The rood staircase that now leads nowhere but which, before the Reformation, led to the rood loft. It was sealed up and lost to view till restoration in 1873 revealed it.*

*18 Carlinghow* St John *(1879). The rood beam and rood erected in 1925 in this nineteenth century church show what was the norm in the Middle Ages above the chancel screen.*

### Architectural styles

In the nineteenth century there was so much copying of the various styles of the past that it is hard for us to realise that the early medieval builders of our parish churches were unselfconscious about such things. They built as they knew, using the qualities of available stone, following the practice of their day, copying, and perhaps vying with, their neighbours. New ideas slowly filtered through from abbeys and cathedrals and were adapted for local use. And in districts of growing wealth there was much elaboration. But the terms we use today of Gothic: Early English, Decorated, Perpendicular, imply an analytical detachment and historic approach that came only centuries later. The special features of Gothic, the pointed arch and the buttress, belong to them all. Before Gothic there was Norman (called Romanesque on the Continent). The transition from its rounded arch to the pointed arch of Gothic was a gradual one.

Broadly speaking we can say that Early English belongs to the thirteenth century and is marked by narrow lancet windows; Decorated, which has large windows with intricate tracery, belongs to the first half of the fourteenth century, till the Black Death of 1348, by destroying a third of the labour force of the country, checked architectural development. Perpendicular, recognised by its vertical stress in window mullions, followed. It is epitomised in King's College Chapel, Cambridge, and is a specifically English achievement. This style lasted for a couple of centuries, till the Reformation, when, suddenly, church building almost ceased.

19 *Lancet windows on the south side of the chancel of Kirkburton* All Hallows, *a thirteenth century church. This Early English style was much copied in the nineteenth century.*

In our area the older churches have been repaired and rebuilt so many times that it is difficult to specify their style. They show evidence of the several centuries in which they were modified and extended. Other parts of the country are more fortunate in retaining their ancient churches little changed. The Victorian Gothic Revival has, however, provided impressions of ancient styles by putting up buildings, each within the span of a few years, in a more unified way. We can best see what, for instance, Early English means by looking at Mirfield *St Mary*, one of our better Gothic Revival churches.

We have already said that Batley and Emley, of our parish churches, are the most consistent in style – Perpendicular. But there are bits of Batley *All Saints* which are Decorated: the south arcade and the south doorway; and there are bits of Emley *St Michael* which are Norman: notably part of a tympanum (the carved semi-circular stone filling above a door) now set in the wall near the pulpit.

The Mother Church at Dewsbury illustrates as well as any how our churches have grown. The nave – see the frontispiece – is the oldest part of the church.

20 *(opposite)*
*An Early English doorway in the west tower, Kirkburton* All Hallows. *Pevsner thinks it must have been re-set. The "dog-tooth" ornamentation between the shafts, characteristic of the period, looks like four-petalled flowers.*

21 *Emley* St Michael. *The lower half of the crudely carved typanum from the doorway of an older Norman church is now built into the south wall of the nave near the pulpit. There is a sketched reconstruction in the porch showing more clearly the Lamb at the left and the Lion (of the tribe of Judah) at the right. Below the typanum is an old piscina.*

22 *Birstall* St Peter. *The lower section of the tower is Norman, the upper section Perpendicular (c. 1490). The rest of the much-aisled church dates from 1865 to 1870.*

23 *Dewsbury* All Saints. *The tower, seen from across a busy thoroughfare, was rebuilt in 1767. Notice the ogee-headed doorway and the concave curves of its pediment.*

One has to imagine a narrow building, probably Norman, its width limited by the lengths of roof timbers which were available, and then the need to enlarge it. The usual way was to build a lean-to aisle outside the north or south wall and, when this was completed, to pierce the wall to secure access, thus converting the former solid wall into an arcade (a series of arches supported by pillars). The south arcade at Dewsbury (seen on the right) was built about 1170 and was reconstructed in 1895; the north arcade, which is of special architectural interest, was built about 1220. Its Early English piers (pillars) have four detached shafts round a central column with shaft rings half way up, unique in our area. The roof of the nave, still with original bosses variously carved, dates from round about the fifteenth century. We have already referred to the restoration of 1767 when the walls of the aisles were rebuilt in the current Georgian style; the south aisle was again rebuilt in 1895, this time in Gothic. At the same time the south arcade was reconstructed and the clerestory windows rebuilt. As for the chancel, this was remodelled in Georgian times but was found to be inadequate in the nineteenth century and demolished. The whole of the present church east of the chancel arch, including transepts, chapels and vestries belongs to 1884-1887. The carved reredos, extending across the east wall behind the high altar, was erected in 1913. At the right hand side of Illustration 25, which shows this reredos,

*24* *Thornhill* St Michael. *The eight-pinnacled Perpendicular west tower is matched by the Perpendicular east end with its Jesse window. The nave and both aisles were rebuilt by G. E. Street in the Decorated style, 1877-79. The north Savile Chapel is of special importance because of its monuments.*

are modern counterparts of the sedilia of ancient chancels — the three stone seats recessed in the south wall for use of the celebrant, deacon and sub-deacon during mass.

In addition to sedilia we have our squints — oblique holes in the masonry to give a view of the high altar (as at Kirkburton), and piscinas — stone basins near the altar for ablutions after mass, having a drain to the ground outside (there is an old one at Emley whose situation suggests the shape of the church at some earlier stage). There were few benches in the nave before the Reformation; people moved about as in eastern churches today, "the weakest going to the wall" where ledges gave support. Old benches are still *in situ* at Kirkburton, and carved bench ends are to be seen in the "museum" in Birstall *St Peter*. But monuments and tombs provide more interest to most visitors. It was desirable to be buried in church as near the altar as possible. One of the reasons for lengthening chancels seems to have been to provide more room for the dead.

25 *The chancel, Dewsbury* All Saints, *is a nineteenth century copy of medieval building. At the right are sedilia and a piscina. The carved reredos behind the altar was erected in 1913. Above the altar Christ is depicted with the twelve apostles, flanked by early saints and monarchs.*

*26 Old benches at Kirkburton* All Hallows, *believed to be pre-Reformation. There are also Elizabethan benches, one carrying the date 1584.*

*27 Bench ends in Birstall* St Peter. *One of the three includes the owner's initials, one the tools of the owner's trade, and one, with a "hexafoil", the date 1616.*

28 *The Beaumont Chapel, Kirkheaton* St John, *contains several Beaumont monuments. On the left, with the recumbent effigy on a tomb-chest, Sir Richard Beaumont, 1631; on the right, with a bust, Richard Beaumont, 1704. The Chapel is now glassed in from the rest of the church so that, with separate heating, it can be used for small meetings.*

**Chapels and monuments**

One can scarcely avoid noticing, even on a cursory visit to ancient churches, how close their associations are with local families. The stories are told in individual church guides. The history of the parish church is linked with that of the lord of the manor and the local squire. Its ornamentation – stained glass and painted carving – displays heraldic arms sometimes with as much prominence as that given to religious subjects. In Kirklees some of these links are recorded in the names of chapels; the Kaye Chapel at Almondbury, the Copley Chapel at Batley, the Savile Chapel at Thornhill, the Beaumont Chapel at Kirkheaton. The Vicar at Kirkheaton recently did a count of heraldic arms in his church and, despite the loss of much heraldic glass, found, chiefly on monuments, the heraldic arms of thirty different families.

In 1547 an Act transferred the property of the recently suppressed chantries to the crown. Initially they owed their existence to individual benefactions; later many were founded by parish or trade gilds. There were

29 *(opposite)*

*The memorial to Sir Richard Beaumont ("Black Dick"), 1631, in the Beaumont Chapel, Kirkheaton* St John. *It is the work of Nicholas Stone whose tombs include those of Edmund Spenser (Westminster Abbey) and John Donne (St Paul's).*

MEMORIÆ SACRVM
HERE LYETH INTERRED THE BODY OF SIR
RICHARD BEAVMONT OF WHITTLY HALL IN Yᴱ
COVNTIE OF YORKE, KNIGHT & BARRONET WHO
DEPARTED THIS LIFE THE 20ᵀᴴ DAY OF OCTOBER
ANNO ÆTATIS SVÆ 58 ANNO DOMINI 1631.
EXPECTING A GLORIOVS RESVRRECTION AT THE
COMING OF CHRIST WHO DYINGE VNMARRIED MADE
THOMAS BEAVMONT SONN & HEIRE APARANT TO
RICHARD BEAVMONT OF KEXBRVGH IN Yᴱ COVNTIE
OF YORKE ESQ: ONE OF HIS EXECVTORS & HEIRE
TO HIS PARKE AT SANDALL AND TO HIS ANCIENT
IN HERITANCE IN WHITTLEY SOVTH CROSSELAND
MELTHAM AND LEPTON LYING IN THE SAID COVNTIE
WHO HAVING PERFORMED Yᴱ TRVST IN HIM REPOSED
IN MEMORIE OF HIS WORTHIE KINSEMAN, HATH
CAVSED THIS MEMORIALL TO BE ERECTED.
Vivet post funera virtus.

also chapels dedicated to particular saints or to the Virgin Mary; modern Lady Chapels revive this practice. But after the Reformation many chapels became family pews for the gentry or places for family memorials. One such in our area, originally a parish chantry, is the Beaumont Chapel at Kirkheaton. Protestants, who refused to sanction religious statues, allowed memorials and did not object to ornamentation as such. In fact, in many Gothic churches, the first signs of the Renaissance are seen in memorials, the work of sculptors who had travelled, or of refugee Continental craftsmen. Pagan motifs often seem to have been more acceptable (perhaps unconsciously) than the old religious ones.

Sometimes these memorials, with their giant tombs and statues of recumbent knights and ladies, seem too cluttered for repose, but these effigies have their own charm as portraits after a time and show us our ancestors "in their habit as they lived". In Kirklees some are in excellent preservation – as in the Savile Chapel at Thornhill; some, like one at Batley, have been vandalised by people not anxious to hide their names. We have, in Kirklees, at least one memorial brass, much rubbed. Above its Latin inscription and the date, 1632, there is the figure of a lady in a shroud and her attendants.

There have been many spoliations of our ancient churches, some in the name of religion in the see-saw struggle of the Reformation, others in the name of restoration, particularly in the nineteenth century. But there remains much to stimulate the imagination, evidences of what religious life was like in medieval times. With our greater appreciation of history, and our concern for conservation, it is to be hoped that none of what remains will be lost.

30 *Alabaster effigies of Sir Thomas Savile, died 1449, and wife, on a tomb-chest with 18 weepers, in the Savile Chapel, Thornhill* St Michael. *It was this Savile who built the Chapel.*

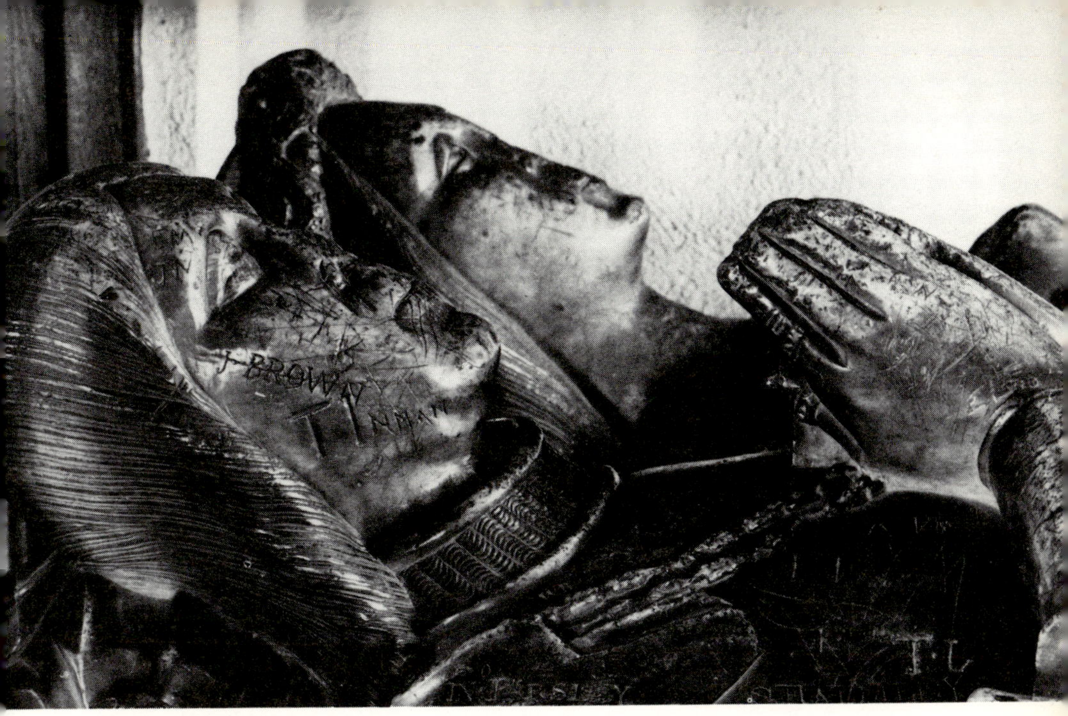

31 *Ancient alabaster and modern vandalism: one reason why, nowadays, so many churches are kept locked.*

32 *This latest memorial in the Savile Chapel, Thornhill* St Michael, *is to Lord Savile who died in 1931. The baby holds the basin, a font. It was brought from Rufford Abbey when the family gave up the house in 1948.*

33 *Birstall* St Peter. *This small memorial brass, now in the "museum corner" in the church, reads:*

> *Here, in the hope of resurrection, lies Elizabeth,*
> *wife of Francis Popeley of noble birth. A woman*
> *of outstanding virtue, she left two daughters. Her*
> *husband set up this monument to the beloved memory*
> *of his loving wife. She died on December 30th, 1632.*

## 3. FROM THE REFORMATION TO THE COMMISSIONERS' CHURCHES

### The Reformation Church

We are so used to a congregation in a church facing east, towards the altar, that it is surprising to learn that before the 1870s the congregation at Kirkheaton faced south, across the nave, towards a three-decker pulpit placed at the centre of the south wall. There was a north gallery opposite with the same orientation. This exemplifies one change made by the Reformation; the pulpit became the focus for worship in the nave. The clergy/people separation symbolised by the screen had gone. Where the screen remained it merely divided the church for two sorts of service: the proclamation of the Word and the Sacrament.

Often the pulpit was placed centrally, breaking a view to the altar. At Emley, for instance, a three-decker pulpit stood in the middle of the chancel arch where once the rood screen had been. At Almondbury, too, a giant pulpit stood centrally in front of the chancel arch. The lowest deck was for the Clerk who led the responses and the singing. From the middle deck the minister read the prayers and the lessons; he went to the top deck to deliver his sermon.

It was important that everyone should be able to hear; close attention was expected. The use of galleries, often called lofts (the term remains in "organ loft"), made the height and central position of the pulpit necessary. The organ, or musicians, and the choir were usually behind the congregation, in a west gallery, or, in the case of Kirkheaton at the north side.

There were fundamental changes in the chancel too. The stone altar, a place for the sacrifice of the mass, set against the east wall, was replaced by a wooden table, the Lord's Table, a place to receive Holy Communion, which was set, at first, in the middle of the chancel, sometimes lengthwise. This accessibility could lead to lack of reverence — we are told that the Table was

34 *The Royal Arms in Meltham* St Bartholomew. *It is the present building (1786) which dates from the reign of George III. The Royal Arms became compulsory in churches after the Restoration (1660).*

35 *Dewsbury* All Saints. *The symbolism of Jonah leaving the whale is explained by a post-Reformation appeal to Scripture. The eighteenth century window, of which this is one light, is behind the organ.*

sometimes used as a convenient place on which to put cloaks and hats — and in Laud's time altar rails were introduced.

These changes came more slowly in parts of the country remote from London. But everywhere the Church became the Church of England and the Royal Arms were given the prominence formerly given to the rood. At Almondbury they are above the chancel arch, a common position. Services were now in English according to the Book of Common Prayer; there was access to the Scriptures, the Lord's Prayer and the Ten Commandments were displayed on the east wall; the clergy could now be married men; and there was a new stress on individual experience and devotion.

When new churches were required, how were they designed to accommodate these ideas? At first, few were necessary; the population was static and the Middle Ages had built so much. Existing churches seemed to be bigger with the abolition of chantries. But with the growth of urban areas, and the Renaissance spirit abroad, a new sort of building emerged when needed, classical in style, a one-room building with chancel and nave under one roof, essentially a hall designed for all to see and hear. In Wren's rebuilding of London churches after the Fire of 1666, Protestant insight found expression; his were "auditory" churches. The new style spread and was adopted by many country squires in the simpler churches they built for their people.

**Classical churches in Kirklees**

Of the present churches in Kirklees only three were built during the three centuries from 1500 to 1800: Holmfirth *Holy Trinity*, Meltham *St Bartholomew* and Slaithwaite *St James*. All three replace earlier buildings, are classical in style, and date from one decade, 1780-1790, in the reign of George III. It was more than a century after Wren began rebuilding the churches of London.

None of the three is exactly as it was when first built, but Holmfirth *Holy Trinity* is least changed, and so best indicates the pattern of eighteenth century worship. *Holy Trinity* stands in the middle of Holmfirth, on the restricted site where the earlier church stood which was damaged in the great flood of 1777. It is unusual in having an east tower rising above the apsidal sanctuary. The galleries required a high (three-decker) pulpit which used to stand much nearer the centre than the present pulpit, but not quite centrally placed. At that time the church was filled with variously sized box-pews and the choir and organ were in the west gallery (now converted into a small hall). *Holy Trinity* was designed primarily for the preaching of the Word in Protestant fashion.

The same architect (John Jagger) designed Meltham *St Bartholomew*, a similar four-square building with an apsidal east end, galleries all round, a

36 *Holmfirth* Holy Trinity, *in 1976, celebrated the 500th anniversary of the building of the first Holmfirth church, at that time a chapelry in the parish of Kirkburton. The present Georgian church was built in 1783; the tower was added in 1788.*

37 *Holmfirth* Holy Trinity. *The small apsidal sanctuary is characteristic of the eighteenth century church which was designed for the hearing of the Word.*

place for singers in the west gallery, and a large three-decker pulpit. It had to wait till the nineteenth century for its tower. In 1877 a chancel was added to replace the apse, and various modifications were made in accordance with the fashion of the time. What Meltham likes to remember, however, is that its first church was, surprisingly, consecrated during the Commonwealth, in 1651, by Henry Tilson, deprived Bishop of Elphin in Ireland. He had become incumbent of Cumberworth and, by keeping a low profile, had avoided molestation, even when ordaining Anglican priests in the area.

A glance at the photograph of the interior of Slaithwaite *St James* shows that it, too, was re-arranged when the choir was brought from the west gallery into the body of the church, for the gallery at the north side tells us that this was not part of the original design.

Kirklees is not rich in Georgian churches. We have to go to St John's Square, Wakefield, to see a fine Georgian church in an appropriate setting.

38 *(opposite)*
*Meltham* St Bartholomew. *Urn pinnacles on the 1835 tower added to the second (1786) building. "Henceforth, by virtue of this tower, it was to be considered and called a Church, and not a Chapel" (The Rev. J. Hughes, incumbent at the time).*

39 *Slaithwaite* St James, *1790. The gallery on the right matched the one on the left before the musicians and choir were brought from the west gallery to the body of the church.*

We have to go still further, to Congleton *St Peter* or King's Norton *St John the Baptist*, to see three-decker pulpits in their original position, centrally placed in the nave.

**Waterloo churches**

More than a quarter of the churches in Kirklees date from the first 40 years of the nineteenth century, more than a half from the last 60 years, and all are in Gothic of one sort or another. Part of the impetus to church building in the first of these two periods sprang from the "Million Act" of 1818 when Parliament voted £1m towards the building of churches in new areas. The grant had the nature of a thankoffering for the victory of the battle of Waterloo, but there were deeper underlying factors: there was alarm about the "atheism" of the new concentrations of workers in mills and mines, and there was the Establishment's concern that Nonconformity was first in a new field by providing chapels to meet needs arising from the Industrial Revolution.

Although the grant of £1m was later increased, the term "The Million Churches" has persisted; sometimes they are called Waterloo churches, sometimes Commissioners' churches because the Lords Commissioners of

40 *Linthwaite* Christ Church. *This copy of a framed photograph, hanging in the inner porch, shows how late (1895) the auditory plan of this Waterloo church of 1828, with its elegant central pulpit, lasted in the Colne Valley.*

41 *Linthwaite* Christ Church. *Compare this photograph with the pre-1895 photograph: the one-room church has conformed to the two-room Gothic Revival style; the side galleries have been shortened on the north side to accommodate the organ.*

the Treasury administered the fund. No architectural style was specified, only that they were to accommodate "the greatest number of persons at the smallest expense within the compass of an ordinary voice, one half of the number to be free seats for the poor". The Commissioners were therefore insisting on "auditory" churches, in effect single undivided rooms usually with galleries. They recommended, too, an off-centre placing of the pulpit balanced by a reading pew at the other side.

The Waterloo churches were utilitarian in character – most were completed, with their furnishings, for less than £10,000. Of several hundreds of churches throughout the country built to meet these conditions, about one fifth were in a classical style, the rest Gothic which was both cheaper to build and required fewer craftsman skills. It must be remembered that though the Georgian classical church is the characteristic Reformation church, Gothic building did not suddenly disappear. True, the dynamic force of Gothic was spent, despite romantic renewals sometimes described as "Gothick", but regional conservatism had kept the style alive, especially in the north – as in the earlier 1706 Cleckheaton *Whitechapel*. It is therefore not surprising that all our local Commissioners' churches are also in Gothic; one has to go to Thornes *St James* in Wakefield to see a classical Waterloo church.

These churches have been described as "rectangular boxes with a tower". Later, the Victorians regarded them as cheap, unworthy, and painfully plain. Most of them were "corrected" to fit in with ideas derived from the Oxford

42 *Dewsbury Moor* St John. *A typical "uncorrected" Waterloo church. The short chancel and the recent extension nestling alongside (the Lady Chapel) should be noticed.*

*43 Dewsbury Moor* St John. *Victorians found "boxes with towers" such as this painfully plain. Here, internal re-arrangement has brought the organ and choir into the nave.*

Movement. This meant, first of all, the addition of a chancel, for the essence of genuine Gothic was the two-room plan, nave and chancel. The two Commissioners' churches in the Colne valley, for instance, have been "corrected". Linthwaite *Christ Church* (1828) gained a chancel in 1895 and brought organ and choir down from the west gallery. Across the valley, Golcar *St John* (1829), by the same architect, Peter Atkinson (jun.), gained its chancel in 1862, but the organ and choir are still in the west gallery, an arrangement which is gaining popularity in our own time.

There are Waterloo churches in Kirklees which remain, in their stonework, as they were erected; they have not been "corrected", except that internal re-arrangement has sought to achieve the same end. We consider one, Dewsbury Moor, in more detail.

The Commissioners, looking at the Dewsbury area, decided that the problem of "inadequate church room" could best be solved by erecting three new churches, each to accommodate 600, at Dewsbury Moor (*St John*), Hanging Heaton (*St Paul*) and Earls Heaton (*St Peter*, now demolished), to cost, jointly, about £15,000. The church at Dewsbury Moor was to be "Gothic with tower and pinnacles"; it was to seat 352 in pews and 248 in free sittings, the general idea being that pew rents would provide for the minister and clerk. In the event the contract price was £5,502. The photograph shows the exterior with external buttresses rising above the parapet embattlement, characteristic of the architect of all three churches, Thomas Taylor. Inside there is still the west gallery which once housed the singers. The interior was plastered and had clear windows. Now, with Victorian stained glass, and with unplastered stone walls, the recently white-painted ceiling seems only to emphasise the rather too "dim religious light". The sanctuary area, described as an "incipient chancel", was insufficient for the choir, so part of the nave has been walled off to create a pseudo-chancel. The little Lady Chapel, at the right in the photograph, now about thirty years old, is the only addition.

As well as the five churches so far mentioned there are also Commissioners' churches at Birkenshaw (*St Paul*), Cleckheaton (*St John*), Heckmondwike (*St James*), Netherthong (*All Saints*), New Mill (*Christ Church*), and in Huddersfield at Lindley (*St Stephen*), Lockwood (*Emmanuel*), Paddock (*All Saints*) and South Crosland (*Holy Trinity*), fourteen in all.

Other churches belonging to this period include Cleckheaton *Whitechapel* which we have already mentioned, Liversedge *Christ Church* (1816), the Parish Church (*St Peter*) in Huddersfield and Huddersfield *Holy Trinity*.

44 *Cleckheaton* Whitechapel. *Here is a Gothic building of 1821, successor to an earlier Gothic building of 1706, and an old chapelry. As at Thornhill and Kirkheaton, there is an inn nearby, a conjunction which defined the centre of the village in earlier days.*

## 4. THE GOTHIC REVIVAL

### Two Movements in the Church of England

The churches we have so far described belong to our first two categories, the two-room and the one-room types, though inevitably we have had to refer to the third category because renovations and extensions made to these older buildings in the second half of the nineteenth century conformed to the new and prevailing orthodoxy of the third type, the restored two-room style. How was this new orthodoxy born?

It sprang from a re-invigorated life in the Established Church. After centuries of intolerance in religion the eighteenth century discovered the "reasonableness of Christianity". The Reformers' zeal had ended the separation of priest from people and had rejected the architectural counterparts, the distant altar as the holiest place and the chantry chapel. But Reformed worship in its turn became formal and conventional. There was a good deal of latitudinarianism and with it a dislike of "enthusiasm"; tolerance was the new virtue. At the same time church buildings were sadly neglected; extremes of clerical wealth and poverty went unchallenged; and pluralism (the practice of one incumbent holding several livings) was common. Two great movements stirred the Anglican Church from its lethargy: the Evangelical Revival in the

45 *The parish church of Huddersfield,* St Peter *(1836). There were two earlier buildings; in one, the Evangelical, Henry Venn, affectionately known as "T'owd Trumpet", attracted churchmen and dissenters alike by his preaching. There has been continuity of parish life here from 1100 A.D.*

eighteenth century, and the Oxford Movement in the nineteenth century. Both have their heirs in the Church today, and, in particular, in the churches of Kirklees. They came during a time of expansion in industry and in population which demanded much new church building.

In our area the Evangelical Movement is linked with the name of Venn. The Rev. Henry Venn, Vicar of Huddersfield from 1759 to 1771, was an outstanding preacher and writer, and a friend of John Wesley. Roy Brook, in *The Story of Huddersfield*, regards him as "the father of Nonconformity on a large scale in the town". At Cleckheaton *Whitechapel*, the incumbent from 1752 to 1771 was a Methodist, the Rev. Jonas Eastwood; the separation of Methodism from the Church of England did not take place till after Wesley's death. But, though the Church of England could not contain Wesley's followers, Evangelicals were not lost to the Church. They were the main support of new missionary movements. Their special emphasis was on personal religious experience.

It was, however, the Oxford Movement that reshaped the churches of England and established the characteristic nineteenth century style of church building. Its essential emphasis was corporate, linked with a high doctrine of the nature of the Church. Though not actually of Kirklees, one famous name of the period is again a local one. It was the pragmatism of Dr Hook, the Vicar of Leeds, who, dissatisfied with his compartmented medieval church, rebuilt it in 1841 to secure a workable arrangement which would satisfy his congregation (which wanted a cathedral style service), his own sense of fitness as a High Churchman, and the recommendations of his friend, Dr John Jebb, whose special interest was the music of the service. Both the Tractarians (of Oxford) and the Ecclesiologists (of Cambridge) had theorised about churches; but it was from a practical problem at Leeds *St Peter* that there emerged a Gothic interior layout which was to become the standard pattern so familiar today that it is easy to forget how comparatively recent its main features are. We outlined these in Chapter 1 – the emphasis on the altar set against the east wall, the vista, the divided choir in the chancel, the steps. Together they comprise what many people still expect as features of a church. But here was more than a solution to a practical problem: the re-establishing of an old style was a matter of conviction and belief.

### Gothic by conviction

The Gothic Revival in architecture was not confined to church building: the Houses of Parliament, formally opened by Queen Victoria in 1852, are sufficient testimony to that. But the new seriousness which saved Gothic from romantic extravagances stemmed largely from religion.

The Oxford Movement dates from Keble's sermon of 1833 on "National Apostasy". Keble, Newman and Pusey were leading figures in a re-call to sacramental worship and to a catholic patterning of church life. Their *Tracts for the Times* (hence the appellation *Tractarians*) looked back to the "age of faith" and to the restoration of the altar as the focus. To them, the one-

46 *Birkby* St John, *Huddersfield, with its impressive spire, was surrounded by pasture land when opened in 1853. It is a typical Gothic Revival church; its architect, William Butterfield, was an earnest Tractarian.*

47 *Birkby* St John. *Here is a characteristic William Butterfield interior, with everything designed to make the altar the one focus. Butterfield never made provision for side altars, though later they were often added.*

48 *Huddersfield* St Thomas. *The broach spire is a special feature of this Gothic Revival church by Sir George Gilbert Scott. His output included nearly 500 churches.*

49 *Huddersfield* St Thomas. *The choir stalls have been removed from the chancel of this Gothic Revival church and the altar has been brought forward in accordance with modern liturgical practice.*

room, congregation-centred church and the classical style of building were expressions of humanism. About the same time A. W. Pugin was demanding integrity in architecture; for him the only Christian architecture was Gothic, and Gothic implied old forms of worship. At Cambridge, too, the Camden Society published a magazine, *The Ecclesiologist*, advocating a revival of Gothic and valuing its symbolism. Did not the triple division of a church into nave, chancel and sanctuary speak of the Trinity?

So Gothic – a conscious copying of the past – grew out of conviction from new life within the Church. At first Gothic Revival architecture was imitative, but after 1850 architects were able to interpret "Gothic" with greater freedom, producing the best work of the period. It is to this time that the few characteristic Gothic Revival churches in Kirklees belong. We consider three.

First, Birkby *St John* (1853) in Huddersfield. William Butterfield, elsewhere famous for his use of variously coloured brick, built *St John* in local material. It was one of his run-of-the-mill churches. Internally it met Tractarian requirements; externally its high spire, characteristically placed off-centre, illustrates the vertical stress of Gothic as against the horizontal stress of most classical forms. In Huddersfield, also, is a church by Sir George Gilbert Scott, the most prominent and prolific of Gothic Revival architects: *St Thomas* (1859) standing in Manchester Road amid mills and houses. We have already mentioned our third instance, also by Gilbert Scott – the rebuilt Mirfield *St Mary* (1871), replacing the pre-Tractarian 1825 building. It was at the suggestion of the architect that the old tower, incorporated in the 1825 building, remains undemolished, though its upper portion had been destroyed.

50 *Mirfield* St Mary *(1871). Another church by Gilbert Scott in the Early English style. The separate foreground tower, at the right, is all that remains of the medieval church, and its upper section is Victorian.*

51 *Scissett* St Augustine *(1840) is a Gothic Survival church with lancet windows which should be compared with those of Kirkburton (Illustration 19). The apsidal east end is marked off inside by a high iron screen.*

Gothic Revival churches differ from the older Gothic, internally, by the domination of the vista towards the altar; all were to see and hear. This one feature from the auditory churches was retained. But the surpliced choir, brought down from the west gallery into the chancel, imitated medieval monastic worship. The organ, too, was brought down, often to be housed, alas, in a way which was acoustically unsatisfactory. The early Tractarians were not particularly interested in ceremonial. Anglo-Catholic developments came later: the altar cross was not revived till the mid-century, and the re-introduction of the screen and rood was later still. But the chief difference between Gothic Revival and old churches is that the latter grew over the centuries; the former, consistent in style, seemed to freeze a particular moment in architectural development, therefore seeming to many static and lifeless. No wonder they often arouse, in our day, a love/hate reaction. But the Tractarians and their successors were so sure of their reforms that when they "restored" churches it usually became a matter of completely re-modelling them, with inevitable loss.

52 *(opposite)*

*Honley* St Mary *(1843). The east end was re-organized in 1888. The Victorian stencilling on the chancel walls, and the richly coloured pulpit should be noticed.*

**From principle to fashion**

Not all the 45 churches built in Kirklees between 1840 and 1900 were consciously designed to meet Tractarian convictions. There had always been Gothic Survival buildings as seen in the "Million" churches, and the tradition persisted. But in the second half of the century Tractarian ideas enriched church worship and gave added significance to the style of building which had for so long survived. What we may call "the ordinary church" was built according to the requirements of the Anglican Revival. We have already noted that older buildings were "corrected" to meet these requirements.

But principle, after a generation, lost force and became fashion – the expected shape of a church. "What kind of Gothic?" was asked, and not "Why Gothic?". The fact is that just as reproduction furniture never expresses current trends so Gothic was never a genuine expression of the nineteenth century, not as the Crystal Palace was at the Great Exhibition of 1851. Nevertheless when the Tractarian influence waned, or concentrated more on ceremonial, the style persisted through sheer lack of fresh thinking about how a church should be shaped. That it no longer implied the Tractarian stance is seen in its adoption, incongruously enough, by the Free Churches. In the last two decades of the century more than 70 per cent of new Methodist churches were designed in a Gothic style, at any rate as far as external appearance was concerned. Perhaps it was a matter of status!

53 *Eastthorpe* St Paul *(1882), Mirfield. The sanctuary area with its three altars extends the whole width of this rectangular church. Two of the sanctuary steps can be seen at the bottom left. Chancel steps also extend the full width of the church, and the choir pews between the broad steps are movable so that a large free area can be created.*

Anglican churches of this period in Kirklees are, in many cases, undistinguished. Yet each place of worship became a centre of loyalty and devotion, and local connections grew strong. We mention only a few features, of varied interest.

Upper Hopton *St John* (1846), more than any other, has a medieval feel when you enter it; outside it is at its best in spring sunshine. Architecturally, the heavy Norman of Whitley Lower *St Mary and St Michael* (1846) is of interest; so, too, is the strange symmetry of Wilshaw *St Mary* (1863). Honley *St Mary* (1843) is colourful: its painted wine-glass pulpit and the restored Victorian stencilling in the chancel add light to its Tractarianised east end. Marsden *St Bartholomew* (1895) also has colour – in its painted stone and iron work; it had to wait till 1911 for its tower. The open-plan interior of Eastthorpe *St Paul* (1882) makes the church attractive to those interested in religious drama. Both the chancel steps and the sanctuary steps span the whole width of the rectangular interior, and the chancel furniture is movable. The little church at Helme (*Christ Church*, 1859) boasts a shingle spire, unusual in West Yorkshire; the spire at Scholes (*St Philip and St James*, 1877) has fibre-glass cladding on a steel frame. At least one church displays, in its stained glass, the Pole Moor radio masts – in the Richard Oastler window, Longwood *St Mark* (1877), Huddersfield; though none, as yet, shows the new Emley mast.

54 *Denby Parish Church (*St John*). Only the tower remains of the 1627 chapel; the nave was rebuilt in 1842-43, the chancel and several other features being added in 1900 when the gallery and box pews were removed.*

55 *Prominent in Clayton West* All Saints *(1875) is a memorial to Captain C. J. Wintour RN of which this bas-relief in oak is a part. Captain Wintour was the son of the Rector of High Hoyland through whose efforts this church was built. Captain Wintour was killed in 1916 when commanding a destroyer flotilla at the Battle of Jutland.*

## 5. MODERN CHURCHES

### What makes a church modern?

It was not till the middle third of the twentieth century that, in England, the question was seriously asked: "What is the best shape for a church?". And it was not till the final third that a modern church was built in Kirklees – partly, no doubt, because few new churches were needed.

At the beginning of the century the insights which derived from the Oxford Movement continued to inform and enrich the worship of the church, and this was coupled, as if of necessity, with the particular interior layout we associate with the Gothic Revival type of building. As the century progressed, however, disenchantment with Gothic grew, for it hampered experiment and linked the church with an antiquarianism which seemed to make it backward-looking, and so, for many people, increasingly irrelevant. The first break-through to a new kind of building came not far from Kirklees – a Roman Catholic church in Bradford. It transferred to church architecture the values of theatre-in-the-round, anticipating, as early as 1934/5, the design of the Metropolitan Cathedral of Christ the King, Liverpool.

This first round church of recent times, *First Martyrs* (in Heights Lane, off Haworth Road), was to a plan expressly advocated by Fr John O'Connor, the parish priest, who was a friend of G. K. Chesterton and the inspiration of the author's famous clerical detective, Fr Brown. He approved the ideas of the Liturgical Movement on the Continent and was decades ahead of his

56 *Battyeford* Christ the King *(1973). Here is a modern church designed for family eucharistic worship; there is no distant altar, the family is gathered round the Table. Nothing intrudes.*

time in implementing them so radically in England. The church is octagonal with an imposing lantern window, and was designed without columns to ensure an unobstructed view of the centrally placed altar. He had already built a church in Kirklees which we describe on page 107.

However, theatre-in-the-round has certain disadvantages, and the open stage with the audience arranged horse-shoe-wise round three of the four sides has found greater favour. This indicates better the arrangement at Battyeford *Christ the King* (1973), our one modern church. Comparison with the theatre is not wholly inapt for, recently, in both worship and drama, the hope has been to secure greater involvement, and the chancel-screen, not unlike the proscenium curtain, was seen as a symbol of separateness. There is no doubt that the church designs nowadays most favoured suggest the family round the table in a way never suggested by the distant altar of Gothic Revival planning. In fact, the two-room idea has given way, once again, to the more democratic one-room arrangement.

What, then, makes a church modern? Not that it has been recently built, for traditional styles can still be copied; nor that construction methods are used which were unavailable in the nineteenth century. Rather, it is that the plan and internal layout are in line with contemporary thinking about the conduct of worship.

**Various shapes**

There has been, especially on the Continent, a good deal of experimentation on interior layouts to suit new ideas about worship. The weekly congregation has to be considered first, but also the requirements for special family occasions — weddings and funerals — and for festival processions. Music and drama have their place, and there should be room for the active participation of the whole congregation.

Our inheritance of buildings, seemingly erected to last for ever, is increasingly an embarrassment, not only because of maintenance costs, but because of the limitations they impose on the conduct of worship. The Church suffers here, as do some schools, from too great a permanence in what our forebears have handed down. We, in our day, are less inclined to impose our views on posterity; nor have we the resources to build so monumentally. Battyeford's *Christ the King* has been likened to a primary school building, a recognition of its functional character, flexibility being regarded as more important than permanence.

The Battyeford church is not octagonal ("An octagonal roof would be too expensive", said the Vicar at the time); it conforms to the broad rectangle idea of our diagrams. A good example, not far from us, of an Anglican modern octagon is to be seen in the Otley Old Road from Leeds: Ireland Wood and Tinshill *St Paul*, where the octagon is of the non-centralised type of our lower diagram. In Kirklees itself we have to turn to Roman Catholic churches to see the possibilities of the new shapes, though Free Churches, too, have buildings which embody the same principles.

There is, however, more than a worship-room in a complex of church

57 *"It looks like a primary school" is a comment which stresses the functional character of* Christ the King *at Battyeford. The right-hand side of the building as we see it includes community rooms and a large entrance hall, the narthex, whose notice-boards include village announcements. The worship-room of Illustration 56 is at the left.*

58 *Diagrammatic representations of various basic layouts for church interiors. Galleries, necessary in days of large congregations and no microphones, are not included.*

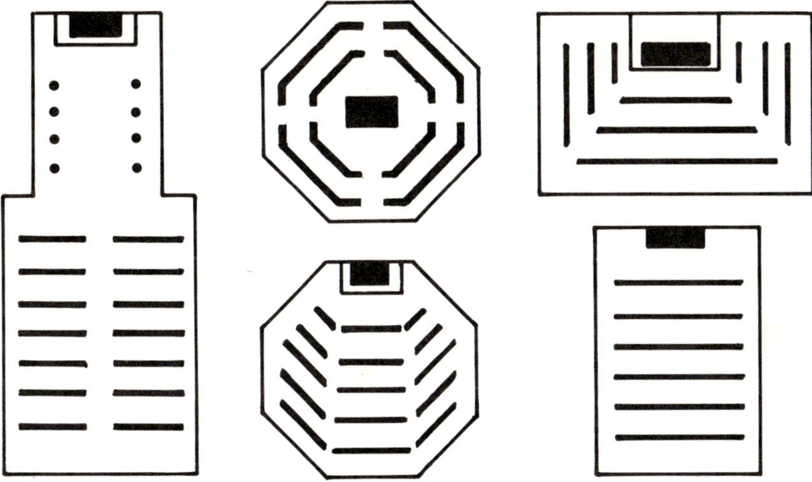

The two-room pattern | The Octagon | The broad rectangle and the long rectangle

premises. Where new building is envisaged it will obviously be designed to serve current needs. Some appreciation of the factors involved, and of the decisions that have to be made, is necessary for our understanding of the few mid-twentieth century churches in our area.

### Today's needs

The conflicting objectives in designing any new church with its associated buildings make a degree of compromise inevitable. What is best in one situation may not be best in another. The considerations involved will also apply to adaptations made to older buildings to meet contemporary needs.

In the broadest terms, the changing climate of opinion in which Christianity has grown shows three phases. In times of religious persecution, or in an alien environment, a local church will be a gathered community, a minority group with a different allegiance from those outside, intent mainly on preserving its witness. In a Christendom situation, when the whole community shares allegiance to the faith, a church can be the centre of a "parish" in the old sense of the term – the accepted local civic, social and ecclesiastical administrative unit. Today the position lies between these extremes, varying from place to place, but apparently moving from the second back to something like the first as the term "post-Christian" becomes more justified as a description of society.

Any analysis of the function of a local church, whether the immediate neighbourhood is urban or rural, has to be made against this broad background climate. Is its main task to serve only its own members, providing a house for corporate worship, and, beyond that, supporting them as they do their Christian "good works" for the most part under secular auspices? In the past social work was a necessary and important part of church activities; today the welfare state has taken over most of these. Is a measure of partnership still possible? Or is the Church's function in this sphere to seek out and define the gaps in the welfare services so that, later, they can be taken over by the state, itself, otherwise, concentrating on personal contacts? Or again, is it possible to discover a modern form of the medieval ideal of a parish church as the centre of the local community, church-goers and non-churchgoers alike, so that its activities include some which are not specifically religious, and it becomes a centre of coherence in its neighbourhood? Certainly the hope at Battyeford was that its new building would have some such influence in its locality. In church building, as elsewhere, form should depend on function, and this latter has to be defined.

One new development, perhaps making virtue of financial necessity, is the dual purpose hall, a return to the idea of the medieval nave. There are Anglican and Free Church examples of this in Kirklees, which we illustrate by one particular instance, Fixby *St Francis* (1954), in Huddersfield. There are older churches which have been re-arranged for worship: some by adding a nave altar, either for special occasions or permanently, in front of the chancel arch; some by moving the choir from the chancel, so converting the whole chancel into a sanctuary with a free-standing altar, as we have seen already

59 *Fixby* St Francis *(1954) is a mission church in the parish of Birkby* St John *(Illustration 46). The building is dual-purpose; here it is seen in Sunday dress when it can accommodate up to 200.*

60 *Fixby* St Francis, *re-arranged for week-day youth activities, has the small sanctuary area hidden by sliding screens.*

62 *Holmbridge* St David *is a shared church, evidence of ecumenical action at a grass-roots level. The church and hillside make a very pleasant backcloth to village cricket on the field nearby.*

at Huddersfield *St Thomas*. From a modern point of view, Gothic churches may be fortunate when, because of earlier lack of resources, organ and choir remain in the west gallery. South Crosland *Holy Trinity*, with its free-standing altar in an uncluttered chancel, illustrates this. Several new buildings achieve flexibility by using folding doors (or some equivalent) between church and hall, so that a large area can be called into use when required. Yet another development, on ecumenical lines, is seen in an increasing number of combined churches such as Holmbridge *St David*.

61 *(opposite)*
*Thornhill Lees* Holy Innocents *(1858). In this church we see a high altar and a nave altar; this second has been introduced to bring the liturgical action nearer to the people, so breaking down the feeling of distance and remoteness implicit in the Tractarian layout.*

# THE FREE CHURCHES

## 6. MEETING-HOUSES AND PREACHING-HOUSES

### Old Dissent

Today's religious scene is very different from that of the seventeenth century where, nevertheless, we must look to understand the beginnings of Nonconformity. It was a time when religious ideas were sharply contested: they split families and communities, and often led to beatings, imprisonment, exile and death. The differences between the major Free Churches of today, Baptist, United Reformed (formerly Congregationalist and Presbyterian) and Methodist, are tidy and prosaic in comparison. Towards the end of the century Nonconformists were allowed to meet for worship, and for two hundred years chapels multiplied. Today, many are fast disappearing; areas of need change, former loyalties dissolve, and resources have to be more efficiently deployed. But we have still, in Kirklees, a few Free Church buildings which date from that time, more which belong to the eighteenth century, and most erected since 1800.

Nonconformity has been described as the overspill of the Reformation. The Cromwellian period – the Interregnum – illustrates best the issues involved, mixed up with politics as they were. Despite the prevailing intolerance of the age, Cromwell himself declared the need for toleration; his vision was of a multitude of congregations seeking truth in diversity. But this was more than he or his followers could sustain; the time was not ripe. The Commonwealth had been prefaced by the exclusion of clergy who, with Laud, had insisted on the episcopacy and Prayer Book worship as essential marks of Anglicanism; it was the turn of the Puritan ministers appointed during the Commonwealth to be ejected at the Restoration of Charles II for refusing to accept the very same principles for which their predecessors had suffered. In 1646 and the following years more than a quarter of the clergy lost their livings, in 1662 about a fifth; some 2000 on each occasion. And so the Church in England had its interregnum too, and its restoration to all that Laud had stood for.

Old Dissent looks back to the 1662 ejection, and to the new edge it gave to Nonconformity. The incumbent at Kirkheaton, Christopher Richardson, was among those ejected, but more important in the Kirklees story is Oliver Heywood, deprived of his living at Coley, near Halifax. He continued to preach despite persecution and travelled over the moors of West Yorkshire supporting many groups of Protestant dissenters.

During the period of the Commonwealth the most powerful form of church government had been Presbyterian: the Presbyterian element hoped to reform the Anglican church from within. But there were separatists also, notably the Independents (later, Congregationalists) and Baptists, who thought of local churches as "gathered" communities. The parish system was not for them. Together with a number of minor sects, now gone, there was also that distinctive group, the Quakers, who looked to the leadership

63 *"The First Meeting for the Public Worship of God at Salendine Nook, October 1689" is the title of this drawing taken (with kind permission) from* Foundations, *the anonymous history of the Salendine Nook Baptist Church, Huddersfield.*

of George Fox. The Act of Uniformity of 1662 threw together these two elements, the reluctant dissenters (the Presbyterians and some of the Congregationalists) and the militant dissenters. Until the Act of Toleration of 1689 all were forbidden to meet for worship: fines and imprisonment were their common lot when discovered.

With that Act, the Church of England, though remaining the Established Church, abandoned the ideal of including within itself all the diverse strands of national life. Nonconformity was legalised; but with certain limitations, and provided its places of worship were officially registered; provided, too, that no meeting took place behind locked doors. Civil disabilities, however, remained till 1828, and it was not till 1871 that the Universities of Oxford and Cambridge admitted Nonconformists.

Nevertheless, for Dissenters, 1689 was a year of rejoicing, and rooms in private houses, and barns, were among places registered. We look at the Baptist "cause" at Salendine Nook, near Huddersfield, to illustrate the feeling of relief at the time. The vivid drawing of Illustration 63 is taken from an anonymous local history, *Foundations* (Mortimer, Halifax, 1933). For the first time the big barn doors could remain open. There had been conventicles before then, private worship behind locked doors, with preachers sometimes arrested and sent to York Castle. But in October, 1689, Michael Morton had come back from Wakefield with a scrap of paper which was their charter of liberty. The old stories are still remembered, the author says: of folk assembling from the few and widely scattered houses bringing their own buffets for seats, of the smell of recently gathered hay and the sweet breath of grass-fed cattle, of men swathing their legs in straw to keep warm, and of the old preacher crossing the moors from Rossendale in Lancashire and reading from the Scriptures "Comfort ye, comfort ye, my people". It was not till 1713 that a meeting-house was built; subsequently the church became mother to fourteen others in its neighbourhood, three in the eighteenth and eleven in the nineteenth century.

We should look, too, at Hopton Hall, near the present Upper Hopton church. Here Richard Thorpe conducted services in his home, throwing in his lot with the Nonconformists after the Restoration. He was a "reluctant nonconformist", and was often visited by Oliver Heywood. The 1664 Conventicle Act made dissenting worship illegal; nevertheless, in July 1678, at the first Nonconformist ordination in Yorkshire, Richard Thorpe was ordained and Protestant Dissent continued at Hopton. After the 1689 Act the house of one of his tenants was licensed for worship. [See Appendix.]

64 *Salendine Nook Baptist Chapel (1843), Huddersfield. This is the fourth building (the first dating from 1713), a typical chapel of the period, galleried and capacious, with organ and choir behind a large pulpit, and communion table in front.*

**Quaker separatism**

George Fox (1624-1691) was not a reluctant dissenter. He refused to conform to "steeplehouse" worship and had little use for a "hireling ministry". Quaker renunciation of creeds, sacraments, paid ministers, tithes and legal oaths was held to be subversive though both Cromwell and Charles II were sympathetic with Quakers. Persecution led to 450 deaths in prison. We are fortunate, in Kirklees, in having two Quaker Meeting Houses which date back to those days.

The old Wooldale Meeting House is thought to have been built before the Act of Toleration gave liberty to Dissenters' worship; this was possible partly because of its remoteness and partly because of "the mild obstinacy of the Quaker when he knows he is right". It retains its primitive simplicity and today evokes something of the quietness and serenity which Quakers found in the centuries following the turbulent years of their founder. Quakers value "that of God in every man". Silent contemplation plays a major part in their worship, an inward retiring to the Lord. There is no preacher and no music, but anyone, man or woman, may offer spoken ministry or reading or prayer. Because they believe in the "Inward Light" they require only a place for meeting; neither dedication nor consecration can make a "holy place". Illustration 65 shows how simple are the furnishings of a meeting-house, and shows also the library, a usual feature. The exterior (Illustration 3), which dates in its present form from 1783, incorporates the building of a century earlier.

*65 The interior of Wooldale Meeting House (see Illustration 3), with seats facing an unstressed centre in typical Quaker fashion.*

*66 High Flatts Meeting House in a remote hamlet still called "Quaker Bottom". The building was originally a barn and was given to Friends at the end of the seventeenth century.*

The second Meeting House is part of a Quaker settlement at the remote High Flatts (off the Penistone road), founded there, tradition says, to escape Cromwellian persecution. The Meeting House remains, a converted barn with added porch, though not all the families occupying other parts of the hamlet are Quakers. But again, something of the atmosphere of a society of Friends is still here, in this hidden fold of the hills.

**Lydgate**

The story of Lydgate Chapel (near New Mill) is the story of English Presbyterianism in the eighteenth century. A small society gathered at Lydgate after 1662, Oliver Heywood playing a prominent part in its formation. In 1672, under the Declaration of Indulgence of Charles II, a house was licensed for meetings for worship, but the withdrawing of the Declaration was followed by greater persecution. After the Toleration Act, the congregation decided to build their own "chapel" (the term was sometimes used, rather than "meeting-house", by clergymen who became reluctant dissenters), and in 1695 Oliver Heywood preached at the opening. The foundation deeds make no stipulation

*67 Lydgate Chapel (1695, English Presbyterian, Unitarian from 1759). Initially this was a broad-rectangle chapel with pulpit in the middle of the longer wall then without windows. There were extensive repairs and improvements in 1848.*

as to doctrine, and "open communion" was practised; the organisation was Presbyterian. Theologians can trace a relaxation of doctrine during the century that followed as the congregation gradually shed the rigours of Calvinism. It was part of the general concession to the Age of Reason by people weary of religious controversy, and it led, here, to the Lydgate congregation becoming Unitarian, as it remains to this day. This drift to Unitarianism was typical of Presbyterianism in England in the eighteenth century, so that numbers dwindled. Revival only came, and then with Scottish support, in the nineteenth century. The Kirklees district can claim one outstanding figure in this eighteenth century movement of thought: Joseph Priestley (1733-1804), scientist and philosopher, was born here. Heckmondwike is properly proud of its association with his early life and of his link with local Independence.

### Early Methodism

We have already referred to the invigorating effect that the Evangelical Movement had on the Church of England; it had an even greater effect on Nonconformity. The oldest Methodist chapel in Kirklees, now disused though

*68 Deanhouse Chapel, Netherthong, now disused, was the first Methodist chapel in Kirklees. Access to the gallery was at the back where, because of the slope of the hill, the chapel appears to be a one-storey building.*

being privately restored, is at Deanhouse, Netherthong. It was originally shared with the Congregationalists, a liaison which did not last for long. Ever since Wesley preached there, in 1772, the chapel has had a chequered history. Early Methodism was, of course, Anglican; preaching-houses, meant to supplement and not to replace the parish church, were kept locked during church services. Methodist communities were "societies" within the Church of England. It was therefore with reluctance that in 1787, in order to comply with the law, Wesley was compelled to advise that preaching-houses be licensed as Dissenters' places of worship though Methodists were still, for the most part, loyal Anglicans. Many served in the office of Churchwarden even in the early years of the nineteenth century. But after the death of Wesley, and over the matter of orders, the severance could not be avoided. The term "society" for members in a local Methodist congregation, however, remained till 1974 when it was replaced by "church".

The great Methodist personality in West Yorkshire is John Nelson (1707-1774), born in Birstall. He worked by day as a stonemason; and in the evenings and at weekends travelled through the district preaching. There is a brass tablet to his memory in Birstall Parish Church, but the more interesting table

69 *Birstall Methodist Chapel (1846) is a plain classical building on the main A62 road from Huddersfield to Leeds. The graveyard has been tidied, revealing John Nelson's study at the right.*

70 *John Nelson's Study, Birstall, with its chimney and sundial. Here, the "pioneer of Methodism in Yorkshire" met people and equipped himself for his work.*

*71 John Nelson built his study after the first Birstall Chapel was opened in 1751. John Wesley came to preach, out of doors because the crowd was so great. He used Nelson's high-backed dual-purpose chair/rostrum which visitors can still see.*

tomb in the churchyard describes him as "the coadjutor of John Wesley and a pioneer of Methodism in Yorkshire". In 1751 John Wesley preached at the opening of the first chapel in Birstall. The present chapel, too big for today's needs, was built in 1846 to seat a congregation of 1150. In its graveyard, seen at the right of the Chapel in Illustration 69, is John Nelson's study, the nearest thing to a Methodist shrine in our area. Outside it, now without its gnomon, is an old sun-dial, his time-piece.

The oldest chapel in Kirklees now in use, and still in a country setting in the middle of fields, is that at Shelley. We describe it in the Section dealing with changes made to preaching-houses by the introduction of the organ.

**The Moravians**

Kirklees is unusual in having three of the seven Moravian churches remaining in Yorkshire. The Moravian Church in England dates from the eighteenth century and was an initial part of the Evangelical Movement. Benjamin Ingham of Ossett had met the Wesleys at Oxford and Moravian missionaries in Georgia, and had returned to West Yorkshire full of evangelical zeal. He invited members of the Moravian Church to Yorkshire and, in consequence, a strong group of churches grew up in the West Riding. A settlement on their Continental pattern was created at Fulneck, starting in 1746 with the building of a church. It is best known now, in Kirklees, for its School, though its disciplined communal life and its training of missionaries were

72 *Moravian Church, Gomersal. The old term "lovefeast" is still used for the monthly fellowship gathering for conversation and tea followed by comments on forthcoming events and an address and, in some places, Holy Communion.*

formerly pre-eminent. The Churches in Gomersal and Mirfield were founded in 1755, that at Heckmondwike in 1874. The Gomersal Church was subsequently extended, the frontage now seen belonging to the 1880s. Behind it the old boarding school building still stands, converted into private dwellings. The Mirfield complex, which included a school, has also shrunk in size, though a new church on the site was opened as recently as 1971.

**Meeting-house styles**

We, in West Yorkshire, have always recognised that chapels are an integral part of our landscape. Older guide-books ignored them, they were despised as "boxlike" and ugly, but recently John Betjeman has shown us how to look at them. Our present concern is with older buildings, with meeting-houses and preaching-houses (mostly called "chapels" nowadays, though in some cases "churches" as if to claim greater social acceptability). They are special to English-speaking peoples, an architectural expression of Nonconformity. In general, worship in them centred round the exposition of the Scriptures in the sermon, with hymn-singing as a liturgical response. Prayer used to be extemporaneous rather than "set". The preaching of the Word took precedence over the Sacrament. The common shape was the broad rectangle

*73 Thurstonland Methodist Chapel (1836), a simple broad-rectangle building of quiet dignity, rests on the hillside as though it belongs. The Pennine landscape would be impoverished without such chapels.*

(Illustration 58), for that shape best encloses the natural grouping for hearing, whether open-air or not, the semi-circle with the speaker at the centre of the diameter. The pulpit was in the middle of one of the longer walls. Usually the communion table was in front of and below the pulpit (though Wesley's early preaching-houses did not have a Table; Methodists took communion in their parish church).

There was a lack of pretension about these early buildings, and an unspoiled simplicity sometimes remains. Cowcliffe Methodist Chapel in Huddersfield (1836) and Briestfield Chapel (1825) illustrate this. Or we might look closely at one of our upland villages, Thurstonland. The Methodist Chapel was built in 1836 and seems to belong to the village; it is in character. Its adjoining schoolroom might be mistaken for a couple of cottages. Its simple dignity and the pleasantness of proportion of its facade would not disgrace a more elaborate structure. In contrast, the village church, built 34 years later in Gothic, seems alien, aloof and detached. Alas! many chapels of this sort have been demolished or converted into warehouses or private dwellings. They constitute an under-valued feature of the Pennine scene.

When Wesley built preaching-houses he had two contemporary styles to copy: the domestic-type meeting-house and the classical Anglican auditory church. He copied both, though he also experimented with the octagon.

74 *Gomersal Methodist Chapel (1827), with its spaced entrances, is a fine example of its period, a genuine preaching-house.*

*75 Gomersal Methodist Chapel. The semi-circular arrangement of the pews, which makes for cohesion, follows the shape of the outside wall.*

One of his recommendations ran: "Let there be no pews and no backs to the seats, which should have aisles on each side, and be parted in the middle by a rail running along to divide the men from the women". They were hardy folk, especially in the winter, for most chapels were without heating! The separation of men from women was common at the time. Later, many chapels were built with two entrances each with its own vestibule, their architecture incorporating vestigially this old demarcation.

The broad rectangle, "broader than long", plain, and eschewing ecclesiastical associations and symbols, did not remain. Even the Unitarian Lydgate Chapel, which began as a "broad rectangle" was re-arranged as a "long rectangle"; to many it seemed more "churchy" so. But in our day the pendulum has swung back and the old shape, "best for the voice" as Wesley said, is regaining favour. It also brings people together, makes them more aware of each other. Many older buildings illustrate the shape – galleried as they had to be when built in a time of expanding population and no public address systems. A delightful instance in Gomersal, which seems to wall in the basic semi-circle, is affectionately known locally as "the pork-pie chapel".

## 7. THE NINETEENTH CENTURY CHAPEL

### Earnestness

The hey-day of the English Nonconformist chapel came in the nineteenth century when aspirations of working class folk were closely identified with the chapel and its activities. The Established Church was too aloof, too inflexible; chapels provided escape, importance, salvation. The individual mattered, not only in the next world, but in this. Nonconformity was also a means of self-betterment. Bands of Hope, the Christian Endeavour, Mutual Improvement Societies – and the choir – expressed this locally; their Sunday Schools (as with the Anglicans, too) taught reading and writing long before the days of compulsory schooling. Members were united in a bond which was both Puritan and full of good works. The Nonconformist conscience mattered. It was one mainspring of many social reforms now taken over by welfare agencies. Dotted about Kirklees, in buildings often no longer in use, or used for other purposes, is evidence of this activity; much has to be looked for in records.

There was no compulsory education in 1818 when the 17 child-and-teenage night workers died in the fire at the cotton mill at Colne Bridge (Illustration 76). We do not know whether Martha Hey and Mary Hey were twin sisters or

76 *Monument in the churchyard, Kirkheaton* St John. *The 17 girls, cotton yarn spinners, had been locked in the mill and the key mislaid. The fire occurred in the middle of the night, an indication of the hours then worked by children.*

*77 Hall Bower School, Huddersfield, now an independent chapel, dates from 1814 when, as an undenominational Sunday School, it was built to provide rudimentary education for children and for adults who had had no earlier schooling. A survey of chapels in Kirklees would be incomplete without reference to such spontaneous growths.*

cousins. Elsewhere there were even younger workers. Dan Taylor, the Yorkshire Baptist leader, for instance, was working in the pits at the age of five and remained a miner until adolescence. Such children learned the three R's, if they learned them at all, in Sunday Schools. As late as 1859 an anniversary hymn at Lindley Zion (now united with Lindley Wesley Methodist Church) began:

Why do we on the Sunday meet
At School, while others in the street
Do run about and play?
It is that we may there be taught
And learn to read as children ought
While in their early day.

There was considerable pressure from the Evangelicals for children to be taught to read the Bible long before compulsory education came in 1870. As late as 1860, at Ramsden Street Independent Chapel, which stood on the site now occupied by Huddersfield Public Library (a brass plaque in the entrance hall commemorates the fact), there were 825 scholars in the Sunday School of whom over 200 were more than 18 years old.

As we can see, Sunday Schools were not only for children. Hall Bower Sunday School in Huddersfield dates from 1814. It is, now, an independent chapel ministering primarily to adults, but it proudly retains its old title. It was one of several unattached, undenominational Sunday Schools which grew up spontaneously in our area; "Union Schools", they were called. They taught the three R's in addition to religion, to children and to adults who had had no earlier schooling. There was another at Lingards near Marsden.

**The organ and Christian worship**

Throughout the ages, as the Psalms testify, musical instruments have been used as an accompaniment to worship. The organ has long been associated with Christian worship; here has been its primary function. Early organs in this country were small, simple and of limited tonal range; mechanically they were clumsy. Their development is closely linked with the development of church music and with the site allotted to them in the church building. In some parish churches, before the Reformation, small organs and other instruments were housed in rood lofts between nave and chancel. With the Reformation this site disappeared and many church organs were removed or allowed to decay. The Commonwealth forbade them but with the Restoration they were re-admitted and wealthier churches found them a place, with singers, in the west gallery. In smaller churches the barrel-organ became popular towards the end of the eighteenth century, displacing other instruments. It was itself to be displaced in the nineteenth century, often by the harmonium, or by the still later American organ.

The Puritan attitude to instrumental music in worship persisted in Free Churches till well into the nineteenth century. When the organ did become acceptable it rapidly became a status symbol – the most dominant visual feature in the chapel. The Church of England escaped this visual emphasis through the Tractarian stress on the centrality of the altar. When the choir left the west gallery for the chancel, the organ found the best available space nearby. Even in newly built Gothic Revival churches it often had to make do with an organ chamber. Free Churches had no hesitation about a centrally placed organ; with their greater informality and their emphasis on congregational singing it was natural to give it prominence. Further, it did the duty of an orchestra in oratorio performances. There was a parallel development in the northern Town Hall when designed as an auditorium for choral and orchestral concerts.

**Accommodating the organ**

We are fortunate in having at Flockton a reminder of the importance of the precentor. In an age of illiteracy he led the singing, "lining out" the hymns (reading out one or two lines at a time, which were then sung). It was the Independent, Isaac Watts (1674-1748), the "father of English hymnody", who introduced congregational hymn-singing to Nonconformist chapels, despite the resistance of the Puritan element. His words, they said, were

78 *Flockton Zion United Reformed Church (1802). This Chapel is the first building on approaching Flockton from Huddersfield.*

"man's invention" and not Scripture; but, as literacy spread, hymns became the most popular part of the service. So, at Flockton Zion United Reformed Church (Congregational), we have, uniquely, a double decker pulpit, the upper deck for the preacher, the lower deck for the precentor where he performed a function similar to that of the clerk in the parish church. We have to imagine this pulpit in use long before the organ was installed, though, unfortunately, the Minute Book covering the time of its acquisition has been lost. The old "lining out", necessary for those who could not read, has not been wholly abandoned; it remains vestigially in some churches as a reading out of the first verse when a hymn is announced.

Of course, older preaching-houses were not designed with an organ in mind. At Shelley Methodist Chapel (1785) we see clearly what its introduction involved. Illustration 80 shows the original broad-rectangle chapel with two extensions. The one at the left replaces the stables where the itinerant preachers left their horses; the other, at the right, built to house the organ, is our present concern. In Illustration 81 (taken from the back of the gallery), we see something like a picture-frame proscenium arch cut through the wall

79 *(opposite)*
*The double-decker pulpit, Flockton Zion Chapel, is probably older than the Chapel; the history of its acquisition is lost, there is now only conjecture. It is believed that the precentor used the lower pulpit, the minister the upper one where he could be seen by all members of the congregation.*

80 *Shelley Methodist Chapel (1785) is still surrounded by fields. Here, records of 1788 tell us, John Wesley preached from the mounting steps at 9 am with an umbrella held over his head to shield him from the sun. He was 85 years old and had ridden from Huddersfield where he had preached at 5 am. On that same evening he was preaching in Wakefield.*

above the pulpit and opening into this extension with its organ and choir stalls. Below the organ there was room for two vestries, one for the preacher, one for the choir. The pulpit is still approached from the body of the chapel; the choir has its private staircase in the extension.

Later, when chapels were designed from the outset to include a centrally placed organ, the Shelley pattern was modified by arranging alternative access to the choir stalls from the side galleries. This made possible the movement of the choir to gallery seats for the sermon-part of public worship (Illustration 82). For some people this is still the expected shape of a chapel though it has long ceased to be fashionable. Many smaller chapels, without a gallery, gave the organ and the choir similar prominence; they too led the singing from their conspicuous position behind the preacher. Slaithwaite Methodist Chapel (Carr Lane, 1870) affords an illustration.

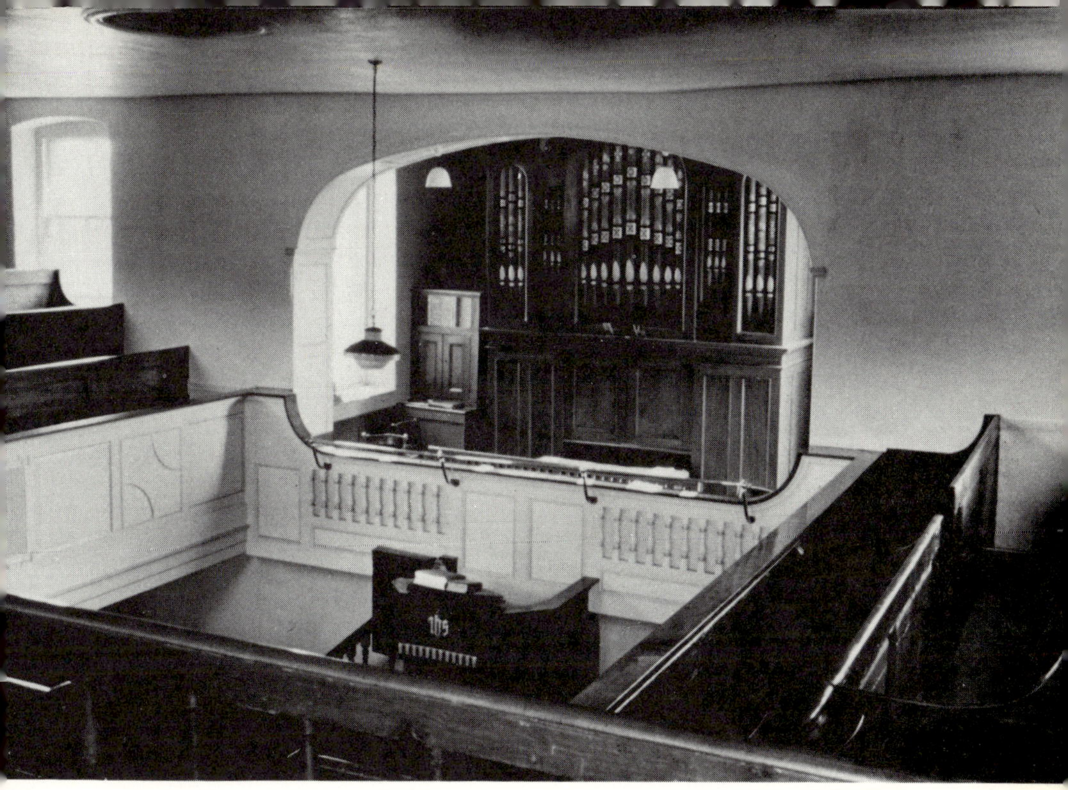

81 *Shelley Methodist Chapel. Here we see how a hole was pierced in the wall of the eighteenth century broader-than-long chapel, above the pulpit, to provide a place for the organ (and choir) when this became acceptable in Nonconformist worship.*

82 *Scapegoat Hill Baptist Church (1871). Once the organ was accepted, the shape illustrated here became the popular one, with a continuous gallery all round, and choir and organ behind and above the pulpit.*

*83 Slaithwaite Carr Lane Methodist Chapel. This chapel, which has no gallery, has tiered choir pews always ready for anniversaries and oratorio performances.*

**Town-hall style**

George Eliot, referring to Methodists in the early pages of *Adam Bede* (written in the 1850s), speaks of "that modern type which reads quarterly reviews and attends in chapels with pillared porticoes . . .", a far cry from that "lingering after-glow from the time when Wesley and his fellow-labourer fed on the hips and haws of the Cornwall hedges, after exhausting limbs and lungs in carrying a divine message to the poor". It was not only Methodists who enjoyed the extravagance and dignity of the classical portico; it was also, and especially in the Spen Valley, the Independents. One has only to see Heckmondwike Upper Independent Chapel and Cleckheaton Providence Place (both now United Reformed) to be sure of the respectability and self-assurance of the worshippers. Anything Gothic was looked at askance; that savoured of the Established Church, especially when the Tractarian Movement was under way. These monumental buildings with their Corinthian columns were meant for large congregations and star preachers; they were built in what we have called the town-hall style, both externally and internally. The great inner-city Mission Halls of the end of the century are their progeny.

The story of the Spen Valley chapels stems from the Puritan element in the Commonwealth Church. Christopher Marshall, incumbent at Woodkirk,

84 *Cleckheaton Providence Place Chapel (1859). Congregationalism was strong in the Spen Valley. The words on the pediment roundel are "Glory to God in the highest, and on earth peace, good will towards men".*

85 *Upper Independent Chapel, Heckmondwike (1890), built to accommodate an expanding congregation. More like a town hall than a church.*

*86 Heckmondwike Upper Independent Chapel (now United Reformed). This huge chapel was filled for the local grammar school Speech Day in 1976, but in early 1977 it was not in use, the congregation meeting in a converted hall in the school premises (1856) next door.*

*87 Highfield United Reformed Church, Huddersfield. Recent cleaning of the stonework emphasises the solid dignity of this late classical building of 1843-4.*

established a conventicle at Topcliffe in 1653 to gain respite from the service book of his own parish church. Both places are just outside Kirklees, but dissenting congregations, formed at Heckmondwike and Cleckheaton after 1662, found leaders from the Topcliffe congregation, including the ejected Josiah Holdsworth, who later became the minister of the church at Heckmondwike. Oliver Heywood was a frequent visitor during their early days of persecution and harassment. In the eighteenth century Heckmondwike became important for its Academy for the training of Congregationalist ministers. These were days of expansion requiring more and bigger chapels, the two we illustrate being the latest in the line; alas! too big for today's needs.

However, not all Dissenting Churches look back to the difficult years of the seventeenth century. Highfield United Reformed Church in Huddersfield had a later origin. The Evangelical vicar, Henry Venn, attracted to the parish church many who might otherwise have attended dissenters' meeting-houses. He exhausted himself in the work and, when followed by a vicar of different views, approved the project for an Independent Chapel, himself subscribing to the cost. In 1772 the first building on the site was opened. Venn continued to show active concern for its prosperity, for its members included some of his former congregation. The present building, with its late-classical frontage and characteristically spaced entrances, dates from 1843-4; it acquired its organ 10 years later.

88 *Highfield United Reformed Church. The interior of this and similarly designed chapels speaks with two voices, as explained in the text.*

*89 Mirfield Trinity (Methodist) Chapel has a characteristic facade, but the interior is unusually arranged with the choir stalls below the pulpit.*

*90 Gledholt Methodist Church, Huddersfield. When erected, in 1890, local regulations required a dignified facade for the new building, with its 720 seats, at an important road junction. Commercial houses can modernise buildings with similar Victorian frontages far more readily than churches!*

In chapter 1 we spoke of "Messiah-Chapels", for the interior plan of these buildings with central organ and choir facing the congregation lends itself to oratorio. The Huddersfield Choral Society's *Messiah* in the Town Hall sets a standard. But *Messiah* is more than a sacred concert; it can be an act of religious devotion also, and many an augmented church choir, with guest soloists, performs it for the congregation. Anniversaries, too, take advantage of the chapel design for special music.

The fact is that such interiors speak with two voices which the Highfield Chapel well illustrates. The ground-floor, with its cohesive semi-circular arrangement of pews, raked towards the back, speaks of "the family round the Table" (to use the language of the Liturgical Movement) and of participation. The upper part, gallery, choir stalls, organ console and displayed organ pipes, seems designed for an audience and performance rather than for a congregation and worship. It speaks with a different voice. No doubt the two voices can be in tune, but recent church design has abandoned this arrangement.

## 8. FREE CHURCH GOTHIC

### Does the building matter?

The term "Free Churchman" derives from the Free Church Federal Council which was formed in 1940 by the union of Free Church movements dating from the 1890s, so linking together the diverse strands of Nonconformity. What are these non-Catholic churches free from? Chiefly two things: ties with the state, and the historic episcopate, both matters of strong doctrinal feeling. Free Churches are concerned with faith rather than with order: positively, their stress has been on the authority of the Bible and the immediacy of personal religious experience. Buildings are therefore secondary; their purpose is to serve congregations. In the past there was little appreciation of a possible relation between the architecture of a building and the worship that took place inside it. Any shape would serve and did: meeting-house vernacular, warehouse classical, porticoed monumental, and then, Victorian Gothic. The main requirement was that the preacher should be heard, and the choir. "The building doesn't matter; it's the message that counts" was a common Free Church assertion.

But buildings do matter: they define what is possible and what is expected, they make demands, they restrict experiment. Yet, often, fashion, rather than

91 *Longwood Methodist Church, Huddersfield. After 1880 about three-quarters of new Methodist churches were built in a Gothic style; Longwood Church of 1904 followed suit, a case of "church outside, chapel inside". Alas! the future of this building is very precarious.*

*92 Longwood Methodist Church. Pulpit, choir and organ hide what looks like a chancel window, but a Gothic shell in 1904 did not imply a churchy interior.*

a logic of worship, has dictated their shape. In this respect Free Churches have been followers, not leaders. This was so when, in the later nineteenth century, they adopted Gothic, and, in some cases, the full Gothic Revival style, so foreign to their spirit. One of the best examples, the New North Road Baptist Church in Huddersfield, was demolished to make room for the ring-road; but we have our spired Free Churches, for instance, Westborough Methodist Church, Dewsbury (1876).

However, the interiors of these buildings, in general, retained the Nonconformist emphasis: the town-hall layout was inserted in a Gothic shell. An Anglican, entering such a building, would have been surprised to find the chancel filled with the organ and the raised choir stalls, hiding, as he would think, the east window. But this was part of the design: fashion might explain the exterior; tradition explained the interior. Our illustrations are of the Methodist Church at Longwood, Huddersfield. Its history begins in 1837 with the usual story of school and chapel and frequent extensions. One extension, in 1873, involved excavation into a hillside so that "the Church was lengthened 18 feet, affording space behind the pulpit for the choir, organ, and scholars' gallery, with a minister's vestry underneath". In time even this was insufficient, and the *Centenary Souvenir* tells how, before the present building was completed in 1904, "the ladies of the sewing meeting were the central force" in financing the project. And the project included carrying the old internal arrangements of 1873 into the new Gothic shell.

### Gothic all the way

As we have seen, many Nonconformist chapels were becoming, externally, more like Anglican churches ("churchy outside, comfortable inside" was a common formula), and many Anglican churches were becoming, in their internal arrangements for the liturgy, more like Roman Catholic churches. But not all Free Church buildings showed this tendency. There remained older buildings, many two-storeyed with Sunday School hall below and chapel above, an economical use of a small site. It was a homely style, which many homely people preferred, and it is found also in the Mechanics Institutes and other secular buildings of the day. Subsequent decades were to see a change, but successors to the meeting-house style were still being built. (In a good many Edwardian homes, the choice when a slice of bread was halved was still "Chapel or Church?", the square bottom half suggesting the old preaching-house style and the rounded top the arches of the Establishment!)

Nevertheless there was a distinct move towards the Tractarian style, especially in the Methodist Church. For instance, at Lindley Wesley, Huddersfield, the first Chapel (1795) was adapted for Sunday School use when the present Gothic Church was opened in 1867, and a chancel was later added to the new church to commemorate the centenary of the old one, the re-opening of the extended building being conducted by the President of the Methodist Conference in 1896. Further, in 1904 the present pulpit was erected, so that the Church now has the divided choir and distant Table of the Tractarian plan, though not the central aisle. We can, however, see an instance of the central aisle at Brockholes Methodist Church, a small church built in 1910 to seat 130 people.

93 *Lindley Wesley, Huddersfield. Anglicans added chancels to the "Waterloo" churches in the later nineteenth century; Methodists at Lindley followed the fashion in 1896, though without Tractarian conviction.*

*94 Brockholes Methodist Church (1910). Here a Methodist church was designed and built in the Anglican fashion.*

Obviously, outstanding and well-known buildings elsewhere influence local practice. The Wesley Memorial Church at Epworth is one such; it was at the Epworth Rectory that the Wesleys were born and brought up. The Memorial Church, a Gothic Revival building of 1889, followed the Tractarian pattern though now it has moved on, with open chancel and free-standing Table, the choir occupying one of the transepts. But better known to West Yorkshire parents who send their daughters to the Methodist boarding school at Hunmanby is its chapel, which also serves the village of Hunmanby, a delightful building on this same plan.

But conformity to the Tractarian layout was not widespread, just as the adoption of the Gothic Revival exterior complete with spire was not widespread; for one thing, both designs were more costly and were beyond the means of smaller causes. There developed a style of building which shows Gothic influence on a basic meeting-house plan, elaborated in larger structures, a style described as Free Church Gothic. And this figures in many of the chapels of Kirklees built between 1870 and 1950.

*95 (next page)*
*Honley Trinity, a church of 1911 in Free Church Gothic, now shared by United Reformed and Methodist congregations. This union, and Anglican/Methodist, are the ones most commonly found.*

TRINITY CHURCH

## 9. RECENT BUILDING

### The agenda

The background factors we examined in chapter 5 when considering Anglican building refer to Free Church building also. We described there the impact on the Established Church of the Liturgical Movement; it was a wind which was felt right through the Christian world. But the eucharist was never given the chief place in Free Church worship despite sacramental movements. Preaching came every Sunday, usually twice; the Communion Service came once a month. A better clue to the Free Church attitudes is provided by the word "Mission", though that word is variously defined. Always it includes two things: proclamation and service. Church premises have, therefore, more functions than worship; they are centres for fellowship and for training, and bases from which to serve the neighbouring community.

But the worship-room is central; and it has to be designed, and the days of the town-hall type with choir and organ piled high behind the preacher have gone. What is interesting is the similarity between new churches of all denominations when they express, in their architecture, modern thinking about liturgical aspects of worship. It is as though current constructional methods and the ecumenical movement were working hand in hand. Of course there are differences arising from the different emphases given to Pulpit, Table, and Font (or Baptistery). And there are differences among the Free Churches

96 *New North Road Baptist Church, Huddersfield. Here is a church which exemplifies in full the various criteria described in Chapter 5 under "What makes a church modern?".*

themselves: in the way the communion service is conducted, in the importance given to the preaching of the Word, in the nature of the congregational stress now given to baptism. As for the building itself, flexibility is expected: it must not define or restrict procedures, but allow for variety and experiment and movement.

Let us, then, look closely at one of our modern Free Church buildings: the New North Road Baptist Church in Huddersfield. The building *says* what the Baptist Church believes: that the ministry of the Word is central; that believers' baptism is a public act of witness. (The baptistery is not hidden under movable floorboards as was a common older practice, but is visible as a permanent reminder to each member of his original commitment.) Organ and choir are there, but neither obtrudes; nor do they confuse the clear language of the building itself. This language is as specific as that at Battyeford (Illustration 56), though what is said is different. Other Free Churches have their own stresses too, but common to all modern design is an uncluttered working-end with features limited to those that have meaning and significance for the worshippers. In fact, the fussy self-importance of the town-hall style has disappeared, and the democratic broad rectangle or its variants, with its emphasis on togetherness and common purpose has returned to favour.

**Opportunities**

New church buildings, like new houses, have an economy and a freshness which are immediately attractive, and this springs from a functional approach to planning. The test comes in use; it may be that a congregation wants nothing more than what it is used to but with the advantages of present-day constructional methods. Nevertheless, because we recognise that future generations may think differently from us and have different needs, there is less stress on permanence, and this makes for lightness of construction and flexibility. Even when the prime reason for building is to reduce long-term overheads, or to bring together several neighbouring causes which can no longer stand alone, each new building presents new opportunities. And even short-term building must be for the future, for members of a congregation who are now young; it is not primarily for those who provide the capital resources.

In Chapter 5 we described a multi-purpose church hall (at Fixby, Illustrations 59 and 60), one way of avoiding under-utilisation of floor space and so of capital investment. Free Churches have experimented along the same lines. Akin to this is the idea of a church-centre, a complex of buildings accommodating many activities bound together by a common belief in the importance of worship. In other parts of the country there are various "areas of ecumenical experiment" where, from the start, and especially in new residential areas, buildings are erected for coordinated use of Free Churches and the Church of England. All such planning needs imagination and knowledge of what is possible and what is being done elsewhere: internal arrangements matter rather than external appearance. It is not enough to put old wine into new bottles.

97 *King Street Mission (Methodist), Huddersfield. The main hall is set out for worship in the broad-rectangle way. Movable rostra, though available, are not being used. There is flexibility in the use of the hall, and to this the white-painted area behind the curtains makes a contribution.*

Perhaps a book like this, which isolates the house of worship from a church's ancillary buildings, will prove to be dated, implying, as it does, a sacred/secular barrier which economic considerations seem to be breaking down. Though optimum facilities for worship should be provided, it may prove that small chapels for private prayer and group devotions will suffice, and that a large area reserved solely for this purpose is unnecessary.

In any case, one new factor is the need for car-parking facilities. We expect to see an old church surrounded by the gravestones of its former members; the new church is set in its own car-park! We get a good example of this at St Andrew's Methodist Church in Mirfield. There are, in Kirklees, new buildings without this amenity, but usually because they have had to be erected on old or restricted sites.

### Adaptations

More common than new building is adaptation of old buildings to meet the requirements of new circumstances. This is how our historic churches developed, usually by extensions. In our day, among Free Churches, it is by contractions.

*98 St Andrew's Methodist Church, Mirfield. Built in 1969, this church stands in its own car-park, a modern requirement. Its worship-room is arranged in the older long-rectangle style.*

*99 Wellhouse Moravian Church (1971), Mirfield, of the long-rectangle type, is much more serviceable than the chapel it replaced in this Moravian complex which dates from 1755.*

The common problem is the inherited too-large town-hall-style chapel. What can be done with it? One of the best adaptations in our area, made possible because several causes were converging on the modified building, is to be seen at Dewsbury Central Methodist Church. Here, a horizontal division has cut off the gallery portion which is no longer in use, and the "area" has been given a low ceiling. The semi-circular arrangement of the pews lent itself to the creation of an open space at the front which could well accommodate a free-standing Table and which provides room for liturgical action. The old organ has been discarded and an electronic instrument installed, the choir taking a place at one side in congregational pews. A disadvantage of such a modification is the need to depend on artificial lighting; otherwise, much depends on how well the Victorian styling and fittings lend themselves to the adaptation.

At Golcar *Providence* Chapel the horizontal division has taken a different form: here, the gallery has been used as the basis for a new chapel, its central area being created by building a floor at the level of the lowest gallery seats. In this way the organ and the choir stalls are retained for chapel use, but at a cost: access is possible only by climbing stairs. The area below the new chapel floor has been made into a new Sunday School hall, so that the original chapel has now become a two-storeyed building. The old school premises, which are

100 *Dewsbury Central Methodist Church. The former Centenary Church which had accommodation for 1100 has been successfully cut down in size and renamed. The gallery portion has been discarded and a ceiling suspended at the gallery level.*

no longer used by the church, have been taken over by a specialist commercial firm. More common, however, is the demolition of the chapel (as at Wellhouse, nearby, and at Outlane), and the conversion of part of the school premises into a worship room.

**The new Pluralism**

In a survey of houses of worship in the Kirklees area, note must be made of the many recent groups that have found or are looking for places of worship. They are not among the Free Churches; indeed, not all are Christian, for Sikhs, Moslems and Hindus are among them. But some are in the Christian tradition, not only representatives of older churches from Eastern Europe, but many charismatic and other groups. In the next few decades these faiths may be building places of worship in their own style; some have already done this, or have adapted old buildings for their purpose. But more significant architecturally is a Church that stands apart from all these, the Church of Jesus Christ of the Latter-Day Saints, which has built a regional centre at Birchencliffe, Huddersfield, and in which members regularly assemble from all over West Yorkshire.

101 *Church of Jesus Christ of the Latter-Day Saints (Mormon). This striking building is at Birchencliffe on the A629 road from Huddersfield to Halifax.*

*102 "Mormon" church building, as here at Birchencliffe, always has room for a choir. The main area for worship can be extended, double sets of folding doors at the back, with storage space in between, opening into a large hall.*

# THE ROMAN CATHOLIC CHURCH

## 10. ACHIEVEMENT OF A CENTURY-AND-A-HALF

### Why the late start?

Before 1828, the few scattered Roman Catholic families in Huddersfield and district looked, for spiritual sustenance, to Bradford as there was no priest in their own area. Yet in 1832, through the initiative of the Rev. Thomas Keily, St Patrick's Church in Huddersfield was built and opened, non-Roman Catholic millowners actually contributing to its cost because they needed Irish labour and many of these men would not remain unless a place of worship was provided. St Patrick's is the one Roman Catholic Church included in Kirklees' Schedule of "Listed Buildings", where reference is made to its "plain single-cell interior".

The Catholic Emancipation Act of 1829 finally secured, for Roman Catholics, relief from the many civil disabilities which had hitherto severely limited their freedom. Till then, priests were still mainly chaplains in Catholic houses; it was Catholic landowners who had been largely responsible for the preservation of the Catholic faith during persecution. Other factors contributed to the change begun by the Emancipation Act. The Oxford Movement produced a new spiritual and intellectual sympathy with Rome, which came to a climax with the conversion of Newman (in 1845) and later of Manning,

103 *St Patrick's Church, Huddersfield, (R.C.), with lancet windows, dates from 1832. It is a "one-room" building; Pevsner refers to its "prettily ribbed apse".*

*104 The Church of the Holy Spirit, Heckmondwike. The Rev. John O'Connor (Chesterton's Father Brown — see page 59) was responsible for this impressive Byzantine-Romanesque church, unique in Kirklees.*

its other outstanding figures, Pusey and Keble, remaining in the Established Church and promoting the Anglo-Catholic movement. Further, the change in the English economy, from agriculture to manufacture, brought a continuous influx of Irish workers, and so of recruitment to the Roman Catholic community in England. The Irish potato famine in the middle of the century added to this movement of population. Irish priests followed, to work in England, for English vocations to the ministry were still few. In addition, for many there was the attraction of theological confidence found in the Roman Church at a time when Protestantism was uncertain about how to react to new scientific discoveries and to queries about the literal truth of the Bible. For the Roman Catholic community itself, a prime mark of the change was the restoration, in 1850, of the hierarchy of the Catholic Church in England.

The story of St Patrick's in Huddersfield is not a typical one. The more usual pattern was first schools, then churches; after all, a school hall could be used for mass till the parish could afford a church. In 1971, for instance, *St Paulinus* in Dewsbury celebrated its centenary supported by its daughter parishes at Chickenley, Thornhill and Mirfield; but the parish was founded in 1841 when a rented room was used till a building could be erected to serve as both school and chapel. The architect of the Church of St Paulinus was E. W. Pugin, the son of the Pugin referred to on page 53.

106 *St Patrick's Church, Birstall. The local Roman Catholic community had to wait till 1971, more than 90 years, for their church, one of the better modern churches in Kirklees.*

At Heckmondwike, the Roman Catholic community waited more than 40 years for its church, the impressive *Church of the Holy Spirit*. The parish dates from 1871; in the following year a plot of land was purchased, the site of the present St Patrick's school which served as a temporary chapel till 1915 when the new Church was opened. Fr John O'Connor, who was appointed to Heckmondwike in 1905, personally contributed to the cost of the Church by selling his valuable collection of paintings. He was responsible for its "Byzantine-Romanesque" design which, with its blending of eastern and western elements, brings to the Kirklees area some of the qualities of old Christian churches of the Mediterranean. Fr O'Connor moved on from Heckmondwike to Bradford where he built a second exciting church which we described on page 59.

**The modern style**

Recently built Roman Catholic churches have special interest for other churchmen because they illustrate the way in which all new church building is developing. We have, in several places, referred to the Liturgical Movement; we have also referred to the lighter structure of modern buildings. So rich and

105 *(opposite)*
*Looking up at the dome of the Church of the Holy Spirit. The photograph shows two of the four marble pillars which support the octagonal substructure that carries the dome. The church was built, in 1914-15, to accommodate 260 people.*

*107 St Patrick's Birstall. It is interesting to compare the shapes of this Roman Catholic church, the Anglican church at Battyeford (Illustration 56) and the Baptist church of Illustration 96; all show the influence of recent liturgical thinking.*

elaborate a church as that at Heckmondwike would not be countenanced today because of the prohibitive cost.

As early as 1903 Pope Pius X gave impetus to the new thinking when he pronounced: "Active participation in the public and solemn prayer of the Church is the primary and indispensable source of a true Christian spirit", and the Catholic Church's authorisation of the vernacular in the mass in 1963 was a logical long-term consequence. Coupled with this have been insights derived from new knowledge of early Christian liturgies and developments in biblical scholarship; both have revealed the richly corporate character of primitive eucharistic worship. Today's local churches gain from this new understanding.

Because it started building late, and because it is still expanding, the Roman Catholic Church has profited most by these new insights; its recent churches demonstrate some of the possibilities. We turn to two only, *English Martyrs* in Huddersfield and *St Patrick* in Birstall. The first is a 1970 parish church, closely associated with a school. It is square in shape with its axis along a diagonal, a skylight providing effective illumination of the free-standing altar which is of white marble; its carved base, in wheat-sheaf form, symbolises the Bread of Life.

The Catholic mission in Birstall began in 1877, mass then being said in the old school now used for play-group activities. From 1905, when the parish was created, an upper-floor church-hall in the new school building was used as a chapel, so that for over 90 years the community had looked ahead to the building of a proper church. An advantage gained from this delay is a church which, in its design, makes full use of recent liturgical thinking. Light and colour are at once evident, and glimpses of the Blessed Sacrament Chapel beyond. Here is a shape which speaks of the unity of all the people of God.

## A NOTE ON CONSERVATION

### 11. THE IMPORTANCE OF INTERIORS

In general, conservationists and Civic Societies are more concerned with the exteriors of buildings than with their interiors. A "listed" building in the High Street may be gutted so long as its facade is unaffected. But sometimes it is features of the internal planning that are of special interest, and this is particularly the case when churches and chapels are thought of; not so much as exemplifying the history of architecture, but as recording the history of worship.

We have referred to the frequent extensions and elaborations of our pre-Reformation churches. In contrast, classical buildings were sometimes designed in final form to complete a town-planning scheme, as was the Georgian *St John*, Wakefield, for instance. But this is to look at the building itself. Regardless of whether or not the main fabric was affected, churches and chapels have often been modified internally to suit new ideas about the conduct of worship. In our day we are able to survey the developments in liturgical thinking which these changes imply. Only rarely do we find buildings which express, unspoiled and in pure form, types of earlier thinking; and because they are rare they are very precious.

No one doubts that the few churches retaining intact rood lofts, and a fabric in keeping, have historic importance. The same is true of the still smaller number of post-Reformation churches which retain central pulpits. Linthwaite *Christ Church* might now be a centre of pilgrimage if it had carefully retained the features of Illustration 40! Are there, then, in Kirklees, churches, or chapels, which still retain characteristics making them precious in just this sort of way?

Perhaps Kirklees is too small an area for such an enquiry. In general the maintenance of old buildings has to be justified by their present use; very few "museum pieces" can be afforded. Nevertheless it is arguable that each denomination should value and preserve, on a broad regional basis, a few of those buildings which are peculiarly typical of earlier patterns of worship. We have one or two which might claim a place in this larger context. Probably the most likely is Shelley Methodist Chapel, not because Wesley preached there, on its mounting steps in the yard, at the age of 85, but because (as we said on page 82) in itself it summarises that phase in chapel development during which the organ was introduced. Apart from complete buildings, Kirklees has particular survivals that certainly deserve to be retained, notably the Free Church double-decker pulpit at Flockton (Illustration 79). For the rest – old pews, tombs, various other features illustrated in this book – many other places have their equivalents; here they are perhaps more to be valued because of local associations. Whether, or not, we have anything of countrywide significance, history, local history, resides in our buildings as well as in memories and in books, and Kirklees has many, both ancient and modern, that are loved and ought to be better known.

## APPENDIX

### The Ejection of Ministers, 1660-2

The Act of Uniformity of 1662 required that all clergy make a public declaration of their "unfeigned assent and consent" to the contents of a Prayer Book which had been revised with an anti-Puritan bias. None but episcopal ordination was recognised as valid. It was the final step in the Restoration settlement. Among those deprived of their livings are the following in the Kirklees area (as listed in *Calamy Revised*, A. G. Matthews, Oxford 1934).

Crook, John. Curate of Denby
Dury, David. Curate of Honley
Hide (Hyde), John. Curate of Slaithwaite (he afterwards conformed)
Lea. Cleckheaton
Richardson, Christopher. Rector of Kirkheaton
Smallwood, Thomas. Vicar of Batley
Thorpe, Richard. Hopton (not ejected, says A. G. Matthews; there was no church at Hopton. See page 68)
Witton, Joshua. Rector of Thornhill.

Associated with our area, but not strictly of it, are:

Etherington, Christopher. Curate of Morley, Batley (he afterwards conformed)
Heywood, Oliver. Curate at Coley, Halifax (See pages 66, 68, 70, 89.)
Holdsworth, Joseph (Josiah?). Vicar of Upper Poppleton (See page 89)
Inman, Robert. Rector of High Hoyland (now served by Clayton West, see Illustration 55)
Marshall, Christopher. Curate of Woodkirk (See page 86)

### Restored clergy

Two episcopally ordained incumbents in the Kirklees area who, earlier, had been deprived of their livings had them restored at the Restoration (1660). They were:

Allenson, Robert. Vicar of Mirfield
Audesley, Roger. Vicar of Batley

Their names are recorded in *Walker Revised* (A. G. Matthews, Oxford 1948) where, after both, the explanation is given: "Ejected for scandal by West Riding Commissioners", (1654, 1655). Others who lost their livings were:

| | |
|---|---|
| Castle, Laurence. | Vicar of Almondbury, in 1646. He subsequently held four livings in Somerset, but "was soon ejected from them all by the County Committee on appeal of parishioners against his insufficiency & scandalous life". |
| Sykes, Richard. | Rector of Kirkheaton – in trouble for preaching to Royalist troops. |

| | |
|---|---|
| Whitaker, Gamaliel. | Vicar of Kirkburton. A. G. Matthews records: "Entry in Parish Register that his wife Hester (*née* Marshall) 'slaine the xiith day att night January instant and buried the xvth day', 1643/4. Tradition that she was shot on vicarage staircase by one of soldiers who came to arrest Whitaker". |

The special case of Henry Tilson (page 42) is also relevant here.

## INDEX

The locality of each building is given by the six-figure number using the grid reference system of the 1 inch and 1:50 000 Ordnance Survey maps. Grid lines are also shown on the *Kirklees Street Atlas.*

### The Established Church

| | Grid ref. | Illustrations | Pages |
|---|---|---|---|
| Linthwaite *Christ Church* | 103 144 | 40,41 | 47,110 |
| Liversedge *Christ Church* | 203 240 | | 48 |
| Lockwood *Emmanuel* | 136 149 | | 48 |
| Longwood *St Mark* | 111 167 | | 57 |
| Marsden *St Bartholomew* | 047 116 | | 57 |
| Meltham *St Bartholomew* | 099 106 | 34,38 | 41 |
| Mirfield *St Mary* | 212 204 | 50 | 12,29,53 |
| Netherthong *All Saints* | 139 096 | | 48 |
| New Mill *Christ Church* | 166 087 | | 48 |
| Paddock *All Saints* | 129 163 | | 48 |
| Scholes *St Philip & St James* | 167 259 | | 57 |
| Scissett *St Augustine* | 248 105 | 51 | |
| Slaithwaite *St James* | 078 141 | 39 | 42 |
| South Crosland *Holy Trinity* | 117 128 | | 48,65 |
| Thornhill *St Michael* | 253 188 | 12,24,30,32 | 12,15,17,34,36 |
| Thornhill Lees *Holy Innocents* | 242 203 | 61 | |
| Thurstonland *St Thomas* | 165 108 | | 77 |
| Upper Hopton *St John* | 197 185 | | 57,68 |
| Whitley Lower *St Mary & St Michael* | 222 175 | | 57 |
| Wilshaw *St Mary* | 116 098 | | 57 |

**The Roman Catholic Church**

| | | | |
|---|---|---|---|
| Birstall *St Patrick* | 222 263 | 106,107 | 108 |
| Dewsbury *St Paulinus* | 238 213 | | 105 |
| Heckmondwike *The Holy Spirit* | 217 237 | 104,105 | 107 |
| Huddersfield *English Martyrs* | 166 167 | | 108 |
| Huddersfield *St Patrick* | 141 170 | 103 | 104,105 |

**The Free Churches and others**

*Baptist*

| | | | |
|---|---|---|---|
| Huddersfield New North Road | 142 168 | 96 | 10,93,98 |
| Salendine Nook, Huddersfield | 106 179 | 63,64 | 67 |
| Scapegoat Hill | 088 166 | 82 | |

*Methodist*

| | | | |
|---|---|---|---|
| Birstall | 226 262 | 69,70,71 | 75 |
| Briestfield | 229 171 | | 77 |
| Brockholes | 153 108 | 94 | 94 |

| | Grid ref. | Illustrations | Pages |
|---|---|---|---|
| Deanhouse (disused) | 138 099 | 68 | 72 |
| Dewsbury Central | 244 217 | 100 | 101 |
| Dewsbury Westborough | 232 225 | | 93 |
| Golcar Providence | 100 158 | | 101 |
| Gomersal | 205 265 | 74,75 | 78 |
| Holmbridge (shared) | 121 068 | 62 | |
| Honley (shared) | 136 117 | 95 | |
| Huddersfield Cowcliffe | 138 188 | | 77 |
| Huddersfield Gledholt | 132 173 | 90 | |
| Huddersfield King Street Mission | 147 166 | 97 | |
| Huddersfield Lindley | 118 185 | 93 | 80,94 |
| Huddersfield Longwood | 102 173 | 91,92 | 93 |
| Mirfield St Andrew | 202 213 | 98 | 99 |
| Mirfield Trinity | 204 197 | 89 | |
| Shelley | 202 109 | 80,81 | 75,82,110 |
| Slaithwaite | 081 142 | 83 | 84 |
| Thurstonland | 164 104 | 73 | 77 |
| *Moravian* | | | |
| Gomersal | 208 254 | 72 | 76 |
| Heckmondwike | 218 231 | | 76 |
| Wellhouse (Mirfield) | 207 211 | 99 | 76 |
| *Quaker (Society of Friends)* | | | |
| High Flatts | 212 075 | 66 | 70 |
| Wooldale | 153 091 | 3,65 | 69 |
| *United Reformed* | | | |
| Cleckheaton Providence Place | 191 257 | 84 | 86 |
| Flockton Zion | 232 149 | 78,79 | 82,110 |
| Heckmondwike Upper | 222 237 | 85,86 | 86,89 |
| Honley Trinity (shared) | 136 117 | 95 | |
| Huddersfield Highfield | 139 172 | 87,88 | 89,91 |
| *Others* | | | |
| Lydgate (New Mill) | 159 091 | 67 | 70,78 |
| Hall Bower School, Huddersfield | 151 144 | 77 | 81 |
| Latter-Day Saints (Mormon), Huddersfield | 123 186 | 101,102 | 102 |

Location Map
KIRKLEES METROPOLITAN DISTRICT
LEEDS
M62
BATLEY
HALIFAX
DEWSBURY
M1
HUDDERSFIELD
M62
PENISTONE
N

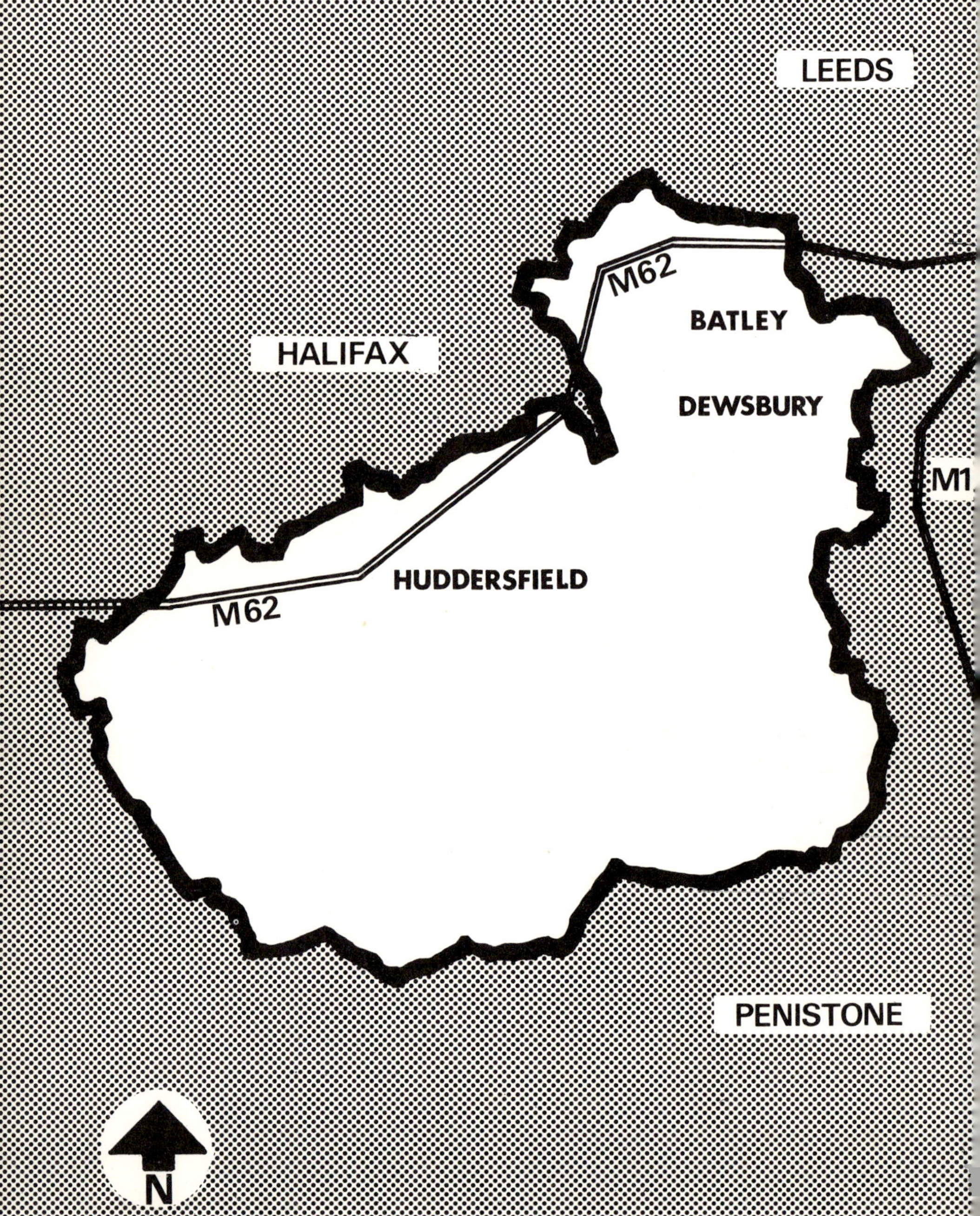

£1.00